ELECTRONIC DEMOCRACY

ELECTRONIC DEMOCRACY

Using The Internet To Transform American Politics

Second Edition

Graeme Browning

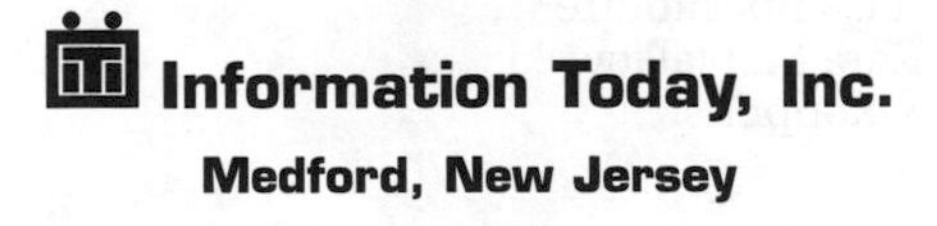

Medford, New Jersey

First printing, February 2002

Electronic Democracy:
Using the Internet to Transform American Politics
Second Edition

Library of Congress Cataloging-in-Publication Data

Browning, Graeme.
Electronic democracy : using the Internet to transform American politics / Graeme Browning.--2nd ed.
p. cm.
Includes index.
ISBN 0-910965-49-8 (pbk.)
1. Political participation--United States--Computer network resources. 2. Political planning--United States--Computer network resources. 3. Lobbying--United States--Computer network resources. 4. Internet--Political aspects--United States. 5. United States--Politics and government--Computer network resources. I. Title.

JK1764 .B78 2002
320.973'0285'4678--dc21

2001047911

Printed and bound in the United States of America.

Publisher: Thomas H. Hogan, Sr.
Editor-in-Chief: John B. Bryans
Managing Editor: Deborah R. Poulson
Production Manager: M. Heide Dengler
Copy Editor: Dorothy Pike
Cover Design: Lisa Boccadutre
Book Design: Kara Mia Jalkowski
Indexer: Nancy Kopper

Dedicated to
Leonard Parkes Brittain III
1952–1994

Table of Contents

Foreword

Electronic democracy was not at the center of attention in Washington, or even on the periphery, until the end of 2000.

True, some candidates looked over their shoulders at Jesse Ventura and wondered whether his election was an Internet-enabled glitch or an Internet-powered glimpse of their futures. But most senior politicians seemed to be aware of the Net less as a tool for incumbents, challengers, and citizens and more as a target for anti-porn laws.

Most elected officials in Washington were delegating e-mail to staff assistants, and those were the capitol's digerati: others who would never let their office telephones ring unanswered never replied at all to constituent e-mail. The Internet, many argued, was nothing more than the CB Radio of the 1990s.

Meanwhile, political consultants were holding conferences through the late 1990s trying to puzzle through the new medium—and learn how to control it. And grassroots organizers were starting to learn the levers of electronic democracy, leverage that was put to effective use most frequently by challengers with limited resources.

Third parties embraced the Net. The Libertarians were so voluble online during the 1996 campaign that media site Webmasters began trading tips on how to deal with the flood of third-party political messages. Then came Jesse Ventura, whose online third-party campaign attracted wide interest—especially after he won.

But it was Florida and the 2000 vote that changed everything. Voters and candidates alike learned how creaky the paper and machine-age tools of democracy really are, how blunt their instruments have become, and approximate the results of what we had believed were simple tallies of votes.

From coast to coast came the call for solutions, remedies more often than not based in electronic democracy. To most it all seemed so new, mysterious, and unknown. But electronic democracy, although still new, has a history. And while much is still unknown, there is much that is already established. Even electronic voting is emerging from an early conceptual stage, with early documented strengths and weaknesses.

The first broad acceptance of the World Wide Web and its unlocking of a popular Internet in the mid '90s, the first digital campaigns of 1996 and 1998 were showing the way, marking milestones in politics and media, starting to map the digital political landscape and compiling directories of useful information in sites from whitehouse.gov and the Starr Report to THOMAS and EDGAR. Political party and media sites alone proved an invaluable resource.

Rather than the CB Radio of the '90s, the Net turned out to be the most powerful research and information tool ever invented. The riches of the world's libraries and the sum total of human learning, or as close as we can come now, are at the fingertips of anyone in the world. And with PCs now costing as little as TVs, and Net access cheaper than cable TV, a majority of Americans have been able to log on, whether from home, school, office, or public library. They may or may not be part of the information economy, but they do have access to a wealth of information on a scale unimaginable even ten years ago.

That means they can register to vote online, sign petitions online, organize online, and vote online—at least in federal and state tests conducted around the country. And they can and do flood sites from AOL to CNN looking for information, especially during debates and on election night. In 1996, 1998, and again in 2000, predictions of traffic to political sites were usually too low when tens of millions of voters logged on to learn the winners and losers and to access political information.

But with information comes disinformation, and the deliberate spread of false information was brought to the surface during the fighting in Kosovo, with dueling dispatches from NATO and Serb Web sites. A short time later it surfaced in political sites, more satire than malice, but Graeme Browning details what could become the dark side of cyberpolitics.

And there are the notable digital myths, such as Bill 602P, an Internet-rumored piece of legislation that would require a five-cent fee for every e-mail message. This and similar rumors demonstrate again and again that on the Net, no one knows you're *not* a dog—or not a law.

And while not even the most expert Web wonks know what really could elect the first cyberpresident, there are early indications of what can work and what cannot—or at least what did work in the first few Internet campaigns and what did not.

We also know the Internet played a critical role in Florida in the late hours of election night 2000: Vice President Gore, projected by all of the television networks as the night's loser, was seconds away from his concession address, when an aide logged on to the Florida state election site and discovered the networks were at least premature. So instead of conceding on election night, the vice president stepped back, voters watched as the recount of a statistical tie stretched into days and then weeks.

Electronic democracy may be the answer that many now seek, or at least part of the answer. Florida, California, and other states are aggressively pursuing digital solutions. But to understand the foundations of what we are building, to get behind the headlines and breaking news stories, it is essential to understand the foundations and the brief but intense history in *Electronic Democracy*.

Adam Clayton Powell, III
Vice President, Technology and Programs
The Freedom Forum

Chapter 1

Birth of an Electronic Nation

> *A popular Government without popular information, or the means of acquiring it, is but a Prologue to a Farce or Tragedy, or perhaps both.*
>
> —James Madison, letter to W. T. Barry, August 4, 1832

The Internet has been evolving in a linear fashion, from point to point, since the 1960s, but on October 18, 1994, it took an abrupt turn straight toward the soul of this country.

That day, a St. Paul, Minnesota-based group of Internet enthusiasts calling themselves the Minnesota Electronic Democracy Project posted a message across the Net announcing that they would host the first debate between candidates for the U.S. Senate ever to be held online. Republican Rod Grams and Democrat Ann Wynia, the two major-party candidates for the seat, had agreed to participate; the League of Women Voters of Minnesota had endorsed the event; and the Twin Cities Free-Net and the Minnesota Regional Network, two local public-access Internet service providers, had offered to provide technical support, the message said.

"This debate is an exciting opportunity for all concerned to participate in an unavoidable societal transformation," G. Scott Aikens, the debate moderator, wrote with a flourish. "All of us involved with the E-Democracy Project are awed at this opportunity to play a role in a larger process which, if conducted competently, will result in the betterment of the democratic process for all concerned."

Aikens's terminology may have been a little overblown, but he assessed the importance of the upcoming event accurately. For all of the technical wizardry the Internet represented, it was still being used as a sort of super-fast teletype, carrying written data from computer to computer in the blink of an eye. Up to that point, the Net didn't generate news or controversy from within itself, except perhaps on specific issues of computer technology. And it certainly didn't offer American voters—at least those voters who owned computers—the opportunity to spar online with their elected representatives about matters of their own governance.

The Minnesota E-Democracy debates did that. From Monday, October 1, to Friday, November 4, an estimated 1,000 people "listened" via the Internet as Grams and Wynia argued over crime, federal regulations, and re-establishing the link between Americans and their government. As the candidates made their points, almost 600 members of the virtual audience logged on to an unmoderated discussion list that accompanied the debates to analyze, praise, and criticize their positions.

The importance of the event lay in the audience's commentary, not the candidates' statements. For the first time since President Franklin D. Roosevelt inaugurated his "fireside chats" on the radio in 1933, and John F. Kennedy and Richard M. Nixon argued over the issues in the first televised debate in 1960, American voters engaged in a wholly new medium of communication with the potential to influence not only the course, but the very essence of national politics.

An electronic revolution was transforming the face of American politics. Across the country, the computer-based world known as cyberspace was rapidly joining the ranks of the union hall, the ward meeting, and the campaign volunteer coffee klatsch as the arena in which Americans debated, and acted on, the political issues affecting their lives.

In the 1994 elections, for example, fewer than fifty candidates for any elected office in the United States had e-mail addresses. During Election 2000, the two presidential campaigns alone spent millions of dollars to maintain elaborate sites on the World Wide Web while thousands of politicians across the country used the Internet for every campaign activity imaginable, from fundraising to organizing rallies.

In 1996, only eleven states offered results from local and state races via the Internet, with updates every fifteen minutes. In November 2000, twenty-eight states, including the presidential "battleground" states of Arizona, California, Louisiana, Michigan, Minnesota, and Ohio, offered local results in "real time," as soon as each tally became official. Virginia voters even had the option of downloading the data to their Palm Pilots, as their state became the first in the nation to offer election results via wireless devices.

The Internet is rapidly becoming the vital link in all of our communications, political and otherwise. In 1983, only 8 percent of Americans had access to a computer at home, according to the National Science Foundation. Today 60 percent—or more than 168 million adults in this country—do. The Internet has in fact been accepted by the general public in the United States faster than any other medium. Approximately 35 percent of the U.S. population had a telephone in 1920, but the telephone didn't reach a 60 percent market penetration for another three decades. Radio took ten years to break the the 60 percent penetration barrier, and television took five years—but the Internet only took two years.

Seen in this light, the first stages of the transformation of politics from off-line to online seem minor compared to the upheavals now taking place. The first online voter information program, launched in October 1994 by the League of Women Voters, attracted only 4,000 users, while a mere 50,000 computer users in California followed the first online tally of state election results the same year.

But these early events are critical because they set a precedent for all the changes to come. Two days after the Republican landslide in the November 1994 election, for example, soon-to-be Speaker of the House Newt Gingrich of Georgia told a Washington audience that he would require that every bill and committee report produced in Congress be filed on computer databases before being released in printed form. The new rules would make that information "available to every citizen in the country at the same moment that it's available to the highest paid Washington lobbyist," Gingrich said. "That will change, over time, the entire flow of information and the entire quality of knowledge in the country, and it will change the way people try to play games with the legislative process."

Since then, the Internet has figured into every conceivable combination and permutation of the American political dialogue. When Senator Patrick J. Leahy, D-Vt., went to the Senate floor in June 1995 to protest the imminent passage of strict Net censorship provisions in a telecommunications reform bill, for example, he carried as evidence of popular opposition to the bill a six-inch-thick document that was the first petition signed entirely online. As candidates for the Republican presidential nomination began to lock horns in public a few months later, a mind-boggling array of campaign sites sprouted on the Internet. Many major media outlets, including *Time* magazine, CNN, and the *Washington Post*, launched the first Net sites devoted solely to political coverage.

In August 1996, Democrats opened what was touted as "the most technologically sophisticated convention in history," complete with an "Internet Alley" that included full-time online "chat rooms," the controls for five video cameras in the convention hall that could be set to give Web users their favorite views of the proceedings, and an interactive saxophone guaranteed to outplay even President Clinton. Almost exactly two years later, 12 percent of adult Americans—almost twenty million people—went to the Internet to read Independent Counsel Ken Starr's report on Clinton's White House peccadilloes. At the time, it was the single highest number of people who had ever used a computer to access a single document, according to CNN.

The online political "firsts" keep coming. In November 1998, Jesse Ventura won the governorship of Minnesota thanks to a primarily Internet-based campaign. Less than a year later, Republican Steve Forbes became the first person to announce his candidacy for President on the Internet before announcing it on television or to the newspapers. Also in 1999, Democratic presidential contender Bill Bradley, the former U.S. Senator from New Jersey, raised more than $1.18 million via the Internet. Nothing like that had ever been done before. But, then, the story has just begun.

The Internet and Grassroots Organizing

In a three-way race, if only a quarter to a third of the eligible voters in the United States take the time to go to the voting booths, a small, well-organized group of citizens can determine the outcome of an election, Jonathan P. Gill, former director of special projects in the White House's office of media affairs, has said. "If you look at cyberspace as a sort of 'fifty-first state,' and you organize it as effectively as you would organize, say, Tennessee, ward by ward, precinct by precinct—then guess what happens?"

As the media, business, and government expand their activities on the Internet, voters are discovering in turn that computer technology lends speed and geographic range to the traditional mechanisms Americans have long relied on to organize themselves and others at the "grassroots," or individual, level.

A reminder about an upcoming school board meeting takes a few days to get to its target by regular mail, but only a few seconds via electronic mail. A draft of proposed legislation written in San Francisco and meant to be introduced in Congress the following day will reach Washington in less than twenty-four hours if the U.S. Post Office's overnight express service delivers it. If it's routed over the Internet, it reaches Capitol Hill in seconds.

Advocacy groups in Washington and at the local level are constantly refining ways to help their members and other interested voters follow the progress of legislation through computer-based updates. Electronic tools to assist citizens in registering to vote, to analyze their elected officials' position on issues of the day, and to join in building a public consensus on specific legislative and governmental matters are already in place in a number of locations. As Sen. Leahy's document demonstrated, it's even possible these days for thousands of people across the country to "sign" a petition electronically via computer networks.

The Internet's greatest strength, however, is its ability to support simultaneous, interactive communications among many people. Unlike the telephone, which primarily supports one-to-one communications, or radio and television, where information flows in only one direction, from a single source to an audience that can only listen passively, the Net allows information to flow back and forth among millions of sources at practically the same time.

The practice of "forwarding" multiplies the distribution of this information geometrically. For example, one person e-mails a message to the operators of 100 Internet-based mailing lists, which are roughly equivalent to free subscription lists for Net users interested in a particular topic. Each mailing list operator then posts the message to the list, which can range anywhere from ten to many thousands of subscribers. Each subscriber forwards the message to ten friends, who do the same, and so on. The entire forwarding process takes only a matter of hours, or even minutes, thanks to mail-handling software that includes a simple re-addressing component.

The effect can be astounding. In the fall of 1998, for example, MoveOn.org—an e-mail campaign organized by San Francisco-based software designers Joan Blades and Wes Boyd, creators of the "After Dark" screen savers—generated over 250,000 electronic messages to Congress in less than a month. The e-mails, protesting the House Judiciary Committee's lengthy impeachment hearings conducted in the aftermath of President Clinton's affair with Monica Lewinsky, were compiled and printed into a petition more than 20,000 pages long that was subsequently delivered both to the House just prior to the impeachment vote, and to the White House after the vote was taken. "We are forging a new way to use the Internet—for participation," Blades and Boyd proclaimed on the MoveOn.org Web site. "After the Internet, democracy will never be the same."

Even though forwarding became a key online strategy in the 2000 election, the MoveOn.org founders' prediction was a trifle over-optimistic, as we'll see. But that doesn't diminish from the fact that the many-to-many interaction that occurs through computer networks allows political activists to reach out to like-minded members of the public without having to spend millions on four-color pamphlets and television commercials.

"What's amazing about the Internet is that I don't have to know everybody's name to find people who are interested in the same issues I am," James P. Love, director of Consumer Technology Project, a Washington-based online advocacy group, said. "If I'm sending out a fax or a direct-mail notice [about an issue] I actually have to have a mailing list. I have to buy it or put it together. And it's often hard to come up with the names."

"On the Internet, however, people find you, just as you find them," added Love. "People have a way of organizing themselves into areas of common interest that just doesn't exist in the more unidirectional media, like the mail or telephone networks."

The main drawbacks to Net-based organizing have historically been the cost of computers and the time it takes to learn how to use them. Together, these two factors in the past dissuaded some Americans from buying a computer and getting "wired" to the Internet.

But the problem of computer prices has largely been overtaken by the evolution in technology. New PCs now cost as little as $400 in most places if the buyer takes advantage of discounts offered by online services. Used computers are available through the popular "auction sites" on the Web, like eBay, at prices ranging from many thousands of dollars down to a couple hundred. Some computer industry experts even predict that computers will one day be given away free as part of promotions for new subscribers to high-speed "broadband" services, much like cellular phones are now free under many wireless telephone service plans.

Congress on the Internet

Nowhere is the Internet making faster inroads than in the U.S. Congress.

The 104th Congress (1995–1996), for example, considered fewer than ten bills relating to the Internet. When the 105th Congress closed up shop at the end of 1998, however, it had considered a record 110 bills relating to the Internet, leading one observer to declare 1998 "the year the Internet came of age." During the 106th Congress, which ended in 2000, 419 bills were introduced that had the word "Internet" in them.

To be sure, Congress has taken its time accepting the onslaught of the Information Age. In June 1993, former Rep. Charlie Rose, D-N.C., then chairman of what used to be the House Administration Committee (now the House Oversight Committee), established the first pilot project to study the efficacy of electronic mail in congressional offices. Only seven members of Congress signed up for the experiment.

Still, e-mail began to catch on. A year later, forty representatives and thirty senators had already acquired Internet addresses, and the same number of members and committees in both houses had requested Internet access, the *Washington Post* reported. Even the most powerful Members of Congress struggled to comprehend the uses of e-mail in those early days. Newly elected Speaker of the House Newt Gingrich's "Georgia6@hr.house.gov" address, for example, received almost 13,000 e-mail messages in the first six weeks after Congress returned to work in January 1995. Taken aback by the volume, Gingrich's staff asked the House of Representatives' technical staff to delete the e-mails, according to sources. Eventually cooler heads prevailed and the e-mails were relegated to a backup tape.

Congress came to the Web even more reluctantly. Sen. Edward M. Kennedy, D-Mass., built the first Congressional Web site in early 1994, but no one else in the House or the Senate did likewise until a year later. In March 1996, when then-Rep. Rick White, R-Wash., founded the Congressional Internet Caucus, only about one-third of the 535 Members of Congress had Web sites. In the intervening years, the caucus has grown to more than 150 Members, and every office in the House and Senate now has a Web site. (Although Rep. Joel Hefley, R-Colo., the last "Web holdout" in Congress, only agreed to put up a site in January 2000.)

Most Members of Congress still don't like e-mail very much—and, as we'll see, their staffers resist having to deal with it. Also, Congress continues to have a quirky love-hate relationship with the Web: Members love Web sites that broadcast their messages but many are reluctant to participate in discussion forums, chat rooms, electronic discussion lists (known as "listservs"), and all the other sorts of interactive activities at which the Internet excels.

A small but growing number of members of the House and Senate have begun to experiment with tactics to build support online for their own legislation, however. Although Congress' rules clearly bar Members from using public money to lobby, a few Internet-based efforts have remained within reasonable enough limits to pass muster. In 1996, then-Sen. (and now Attorney General) John Ashcroft, R-Mo., became the first Senate member to launch an online petition, in support of a term limits bill. The petition collected 7,100 signatures in less than two weeks. Since 1999, both House Majority Leader Richard Armey of Texas and House Minority Leader Richard Gephardt of Missouri have maintained Web sites presenting arguments and proposals for opposing tax plans. Both sites urge visitors to sign up for electronic mailing lists that provide regular updates on how the tax measures are faring.

"A lot of people are still in the traditional mindset. They think, 'We've got to use a mailing to get the message across,'" Richard Diamond, Armey's press secretary and Webmaster for the Congressional site, told the *New York Times*. "What they don't see is [that] e-mail is more effective, and it doesn't cost anything, and it reaches a targeted audience."

If there are any doubts that Congress now "gets it" as far as the Internet itself is concerned, however, House Speaker Dennis Hastert of Illinois put them to rest in a recent "Dear Colleague" letter to House Republicans. "Whether we are speaking in such terminology as 'digital age,' 'information superhighway,' or the 'knowledge economy,'" Hastert wrote, "the success of the Internet is real and it is here."

Looking Ahead

For a medium originally developed as a "command, control, and communication" device for the Pentagon to maintain links between Congress, the White House, and the military in the event of a nuclear war, the Internet has developed a nonhierarchical internal structure. What began, in 1969, as ARPANet—named for the Pentagon's Advanced Research Projects Agency—at four university sites in California and Utah, has now become a vast web of computer networks linked all over the world. Where access to this network was once limited to computer scientists at prestigious universities, anyone can now send messages, tap into databases, and discuss every topic under the sun. All it takes is a computer, a modem, and a connection through an Internet service provider or a commercial online service such as America Online.

Internet technology is also evolving so rapidly that users of more-advanced computers can transmit data to other users that have the same emotional, see-it-now impact as television. Before the advent of the Web, the Internet could only deliver text from one computer to another. On the Web, however, information travels with sound and full-color pictures or video as well as text. It's as close to television as computers have ever come, but it costs a fraction of the normal fee for air time. "Streaming video," the newest technological wonder to hit the Net, even brings the lights-cameras-action element of motion pictures to the screens of users who have broadband access.

At the same time, the Internet audience—once a group known primarily for its homogeneity—now resembles mainstream America. "Increasingly people without college training, those with modest incomes, and women are joining the ranks of Internet users, who not long ago were largely well educated, affluent men," the Pew Research Center for the People and the Press reported in 1998. African-Americans, Hispanic Americans, and Asian-Americans also now represent significant segments of the Net community, although there is conflicting research about the depth of the "digital divide" in this country.

Net regulars tend to be vitally interested in political issues. Some 45 percent of those Americans who have used the Internet for three years or more go online to learn about candidates and election news, the Pew Research Center reported in early December 2000. While some politicians would characterize the Internet as a bastion of far-left ideology, there is evidence that Americans who go online are no more partisan than other citizens. A 1995 study of technology in the American household by the Times Mirror Center for the People & the Press found that computer users are almost identical to those who don't use a computer in terms of party identification and congressional and presidential voting patterns.

Political operatives in Washington are well aware of these statistics. "The guys who use the Web were the swing vote," Tom Gibson, a partner in the Wexler Group, a powerful Washington lobbying firm, said shortly after the 1992 presidential election. "Those are the people you want to reach in 1996, and beyond."

"From 1992 to 1996, we saw an explosion in the percentage of the general population who were on the Internet—so much so that in this election cycle the Internet has reached the same capacity as mail and radio to reach a very specific demographic of the electorate in a cost-effective and meaningful way. It takes a level of computer and technical literacy to get online, and, because of that, these are the kinds of voters you want to reach with an intelligent and a well-defined message," said Robert K. Arena, Jr., who was director of Internet strategy for the Dole campaign in 1996, and an advisor to the Republican National

Committee on its Internet strategy for the 2000 elections. "As we move beyond 2000, Internet users will represent a more and more active segment of the population, and, as such, politicians can't afford to bypass reaching out to those voters in the medium they're most comfortable with."

As the Net's politically oriented community grows and changes, it may take the Internet in directions that its original founders never thought possible. For example, Ben Brink, a Republican from Silicon Valley who ran the first wholly online congressional campaign in 1994, promised voters that he would try to pass legislation requiring congressional committee hearings to be conducted via videoconferencing, so that members of Congress could spend more time in their home districts. That idea has yet to be tested, but with the coming of high-speed, high-volume broadband and cable services to the Internet, videoconferences for committee hearings could be commonplace some day. In late February 1996, President Clinton gave the first presidential speech ever broadcast over computer networks in the interactive CUSeeMe format developed by Cornell University. The broadcast was far from watchable—even at fifty-six kilobytes-per-second, the fastest modem speed generally available at the time, the images jerked and the audio quality was spotty—but it signaled a monumental break from the "old" one-to-many communications format in which television dominates. As if to prove that very point, three and one-half years later, in November 1999, Clinton hosted a "virtual town hall meeting" with an estimated 30,000 elected officials and citizens from across the country. Those who watched and listened to the event via the Internet were also encouraged to e-mail questions to the President, who then chose which questions to answer from a list that scrolled up on a nearby computer screen. For the first time Americans had the opportunity to communicate directly and spontaneously with the nation's Chief Executive without regard to geographic limits.

One of the online community's favorite pastimes is musing over which software program, or "application," will eventually raise the Net out of the world of the privileged and computer savvy into the broad public realm. While politics isn't a software program by any stretch of the imagination, political debate could make the Internet as much a fixture in American households as telephones and television already are.

Politics is already one of the fastest-growing corners of the Web. In early 1996, two years after the Minnesota E-Democracy debates took place, Stardot Consulting of Boulder, Colorado, announced that it was opening its doors as the first political consulting firm to focus entirely on Internet-based campaigns. At the same time, Yahoo!, the popular Internet search engine, listed more than 390 Web sites devoted to political forums, interest groups, organizations, and parties, as well as general information for voters. Four years later, during the 2000 presidential election, Yahoo! listed more than 2,800 such sites. Nowadays, a search of the membership roster for the Communications and Policy Technology Network, a Washington, D.C.-based organization for online political consultants, reveals more than 100 people who specialize in such Internet-centric services as online fundraising, lobbying, and organizing, and "e-mail campaigns."

Unfortunately, some traditional politicians still don't seem to understand this. Congress' presence on the Internet consists, in the main, of flashy home pages that tout Members' accomplishments but do little to gather feedback from constituents. Even those Members brave enough to accept e-mail tend to carry on one-way electronic communication, responding to e-mail queries with paper letters delivered through the regular mail. Most state and local lawmakers' Web sites and e-mail practices are even worse—if the sites and addresses exist at all.

The terrorist attacks of September 11, 2001 have encouraged at least some members of Congress to take a fresh look at the benefits of electronic communication. On Dec. 6, 2001, Rep. Jim Langevin (D-R.I.), a Congressional newcomer, introduced a bill to require the National Institutes of Standards and Technology to study the feasibility and cost of creating a communications system that would allow Congress to vote from remote locations in the event of another devastating terrorist attack. Langevin's legislation would permit Congress to vote electronically "if circumstances require [it] to convene without being at a single location."

Langevin's bill offers hope for a more enlightened approach in Congress, but those schooled in traditional politics still tend to see the Internet as little more than a big electronic auditorium where millions of people gather to spout off much like high-school kids in a civics class—but nonetheless have little actual impact on the crafting of policies that govern them. This vision simply rationalizes the use of old messages in a new medium. "I'll give you several proposals and you tell me which one you like the best. I'm here to listen," the lawmaker says to the public in the traditional scheme. The problem is that the proposals have already been crafted in some private meeting, where the public could attend only through the representation of pricey lobbyists.

Better that the Internet's power be put to work building consensus via information passed back and forth between citizens at times that are convenient for them. "The less that electronic democracy proposals are focused upon real-time applications—watching a TV show and pushing some buttons—the more likely it is that what is proposed will take advantage of one of the key contributions interactivity is able to make," former White House staffer David A. Lytel wrote in *Media Regimes and Political Communication: Democracy and Interactive Media in France*. "The promise of a new interactive regime lies in harnessing the power of the activists to educate and motivate their fellow citizens, rather than focusing their resources upon influencing legislators."

More and more Internet-savvy Americans are "educating and motivating" their fellow citizens these days on every political issue under the sun. If you've got an issue that you think lawmakers should address, you can do the same.

Chapter 2

Smoke-Filled Rooms in Cyberspace

The more I see of it, the more I slowly come to believe that the massive information processing power which has traditionally been available only to the rich and powerful in government and large corporations will truly become available to the general public. And I see that as having a tremendous democratizing potential, for most assuredly, information—data and the ability to organize and process it—is power. It is an exciting vision to me.

—Jim Clark Warren, Jr., Founder of *Dr. Dobb's Journal of Computer Calisthenics & Orthodontia*, in his preface to the first edition in 1976

At a 1995 panel discussion in Washington on the subject of Congress and the "new media," I spoke—rather eloquently, I thought—about how important it was for Capitol Hill to recognize the growing presence of the online community. When the discussion ended, a distinguished political scientist from Rutgers University who had also been on the panel leaned over to me. "I was interested in your views," he said, "but isn't all this Internet stuff a fad—sort of the CB radio of the '90s?"

I don't believe this was a flippant question. The professor had too serious a look on his face for me to think he was joking. Besides, I'd heard versions of the same query before, often from very influential lawmakers. Despite statistics showing that—even then!—more Americans than ever not only owned computers, but were also using them to affect everything from business and education to science and the arts, the amorphous world of cyberspace was as alien to most political power players as was the landscape of Mars.

If you asked members of Congress and their aides why this was so, they could give a number of reasons. Computers are complex machines, and it takes time to learn how to use them, they would say. Navigating the Internet can be confusing at first, even with Web browsers. There's so much information out there it's hard to know where to start. And after all, when a lawmaker has to tend to daily crises involving issues like homelessness and crime, learning how to respond to e-mail falls to the bottom of the priority list.

That last excuse was the only realistic one in 1995. Internet technology was still so unsophisticated then that most voters would likely have preferred that their elected representatives try to solve the great problems of the country than struggling with a URL that didn't respond. Few people would have disagreed with the argument that it made more sense for a staff aide to do the work of mastering the Net and passing constituent inquiries and comments up through the interoffice chain of command, while the lawmaker did the job he or she was elected to do.

But I suspected in those early days that the reason many politicians didn't take much notice of their Net constituency was because of the perception in Washington, and around the country, that the Internet didn't represent a political force to be reckoned with.

Even in the latter part of the twentieth century and the dawn of the twenty-first, many people still consider politics a zero-sum game. Somebody wins and somebody loses. The vote margin may be razor thin and the moral authority may rest wholly with one side and not the other, but some person or proposal still ends up the victor and the rest are also-rans. The tendency to view the political process in all its incarnations as a series of horse races thrives, particularly in Washington. The public often blames the press for fostering the horse-race mentality in the political arena, but the zero-sum perspective in Washington would exist just fine on its own even if every newspaper and television network disappeared from the face of the earth. "Who won?" is such a common question around Capitol Hill that it has become a term of art.

It may still be too early to predict how and when the Internet will truly change the rules of American politics. But Net-based organizing, lobbying, consensus building, and advocacy—the basic elements of political life in this country—have been occurring for far longer than today's dot-com "political Web sites" would have you believe. Internet-based activists of all political stripes were helping to pass laws, change or halt legislative proposals, and steer the course of campaigns even in the days when the World Wide Web existed only as white text on a black background. These people were the pioneers of our burgeoning electronic democracy—but their exploits were only the beginning.

Putting the California Legislature Online

Jim Warren was one of the first settlers in cyberspace, and he's always had a vision of the brave new world that it represents. In 1976, he founded *Dr. Dobb's Journal of Computer Calisthenics & Orthodontia*, a photocopied newsletter that went out to the few hundred personal computer enthusiasts who existed in the United States at the time. Eventually the newsletter became one of the first full-fledged magazines devoted to PCs, and "Dr. Dobb's" became a byword in the growing online community for unassailable analyses of computer technology.

Meanwhile, Warren, who had completed two advanced degrees in computer programming, began teaching computer science at Stanford University. In 1977, he organized the first West Coast Computer Faire, an idiosyncratic gathering of computer hardware makers, software developers, and electronic game aficionados that the *New York Times* once called a "twentieth-century technological rerun of the market fairs that made Hanover and the other great German cities postmedieval centers of commerce." In 1983, at the last fair he organized, Warren "glided effortlessly and efficiently through the crowds on roller skates," explaining that his mode of

Figure 2.1 Jim Warren told California legislative staffers, "Trust me, there's a cheap way to do this!"

transportation "may not be traditional, but it's practical, and that's what microcomputing is all about," the *Times* reported.

Warren, a large, bearded man whose impish behavior disguises an incisive mind, also began writing monthly columns for *MicroTimes* and *Government Technology*, two magazines read primarily by the operators of computer bulletin boards.

In the 1980s, while scientists and university researchers traded Socratic dialogues on ARPANet, ordinary citizens logged on to bulletin board systems, or BBSs, for digital chitchat and information. A BBS is really nothing more than a computer outfitted with software that accepts information from, and sends information to, other computers, and a modem that makes that data transfer possible via the telephone lines. Just about anyone who has a computer can set up a BBS, and starting in the early '80s thousands of people did. The systems became known as "bulletin boards" because the more computer users dialed in to post messages and swap information, the more the systems' screens would come to resemble a corkboard in the neighborhood grocery store, covered with handwritten notes, brightly colored fliers, and pictures of household items for sale.

Computer users flocked to BBSs throughout the decade because they offered the sort of communal dialogue and sharing of interests that make the large commercial online services like America Online and Prodigy so popular today. Since the Internet was still not widely accessible, BBSs also became repositories of information on a variety of subjects that interested the public. Over the years, Warren wrote a number of magazine columns arguing that government information and public records were ideally suited to storage in a similar online format.

He reiterated his arguments at the many conferences where he was invited to speak. One day in early March 1993, a California state official with whom Warren had recently shared the podium faxed him a copy of a bill that Debra Bowen, a Democrat from Marina del Rey, California, and a first-time member of the California State Assembly, had just introduced. The measure required an account of bills introduced, votes, committee analyses, debates, and other legislative activity to be uploaded to the Internet at the close of every day the legislature was in session. It also directed the legislature's Office of Legislative Counsel to make the California constitution, the state code, and daily floor and committee agendas available online. In essence, the Bowen bill gave citizens computer access to the same information they could obtain on paper from the legislature.

Warren wrote approvingly about the bill in his *MicroTimes* column. Several days later, almost on a whim, he faxed a copy of the column to Bowen's office.

An hour later, a Bowen staffer called to thank Warren for his support. The staffer cautioned, however, that the bill had little chance of passage because the State Assembly's Legislative Data Center had recommended that the state build its own statewide computer network to distribute the information, an undertaking that would cost millions. More important, Bowen and her staff "didn't know of any support bases for such legislation," Warren explained in a recent e-mail message. "I blurted out, 'Well, why don't you just use a desktop file-server and the Internet?' The staffer asked, 'Uh, what's that?' I said, 'Trust me; there's a cheap way to do this!'"

That night Warren posted messages about the Bowen bill all over the Internet and to every BBS he knew. Within a few days, Bowen's staff had a handful of letters and faxes from citizens supporting the bill—enough to give the measure plenty of positive political momentum, according to Warren.

However, the bill drew mixed reactions from members of the legislature's powerful Rules Committee when it was first heard. Some lawmakers complained that private companies that maintained databases of state information might pull out of their contracts, causing the state to lose valuable revenue. Others were skeptical that the public would be interested in unfiltered legislative data, or that computer neophytes would venture onto the Internet, whose byways were much more difficult to use back then, just for the sake of a voting record or two. A few lawmakers even suggested that the information should be copyrighted, so that computer users would have to pay the state a fee to download it.

All the while an online coalition of voters, community leaders, reporters, radio talk-show hosts, businesses such as Apple Computer Corp., and advocacy organizations such as the League of Women Voters and the Sierra Club monitored the bill's day-to-day progress via an e-mail distribution list that Warren had organized. A regular mail, or "snail mail," list and a telephone "tree," where designated volunteers agreed to call other volunteers with legislative alerts, kept the noncomputerized segment of the bill's supporters up-to-date.

Opponents argued that the bill wouldn't serve nearly as many California citizens as Warren and other supporters believed. "You're looking at an elite group of people being able to use the Internet," Sheryl Bell, manager for a company called Legitech, told the *California Journal Weekly*, a Sacramento-based political newspaper. "That, to me, doesn't seem like public access."

Bowen was adamant. "Californians already pay $50 million a year to create, operate, and manage this information," she told the *Los Angeles Times*. "They shouldn't have to pay a second fee to see what they've already paid to create."

Warren kept up the pressure, traveling often from his home thirty miles outside of San Francisco to Sacramento to consult with Bowen's staff. At their urging, he presented a plan to distribute the information on the Internet to top administrators at the Legislative Data Center.

Later, he wrote an eighteen-page analysis of the Internet-based distribution plan at the request of the chairman of the Rules Committee.

Whenever a hearing or a vote on the bill approached, Warren would issue electronic "action alerts" to supporters via the Internet as well as through postal mailings and alerts to the telephone tree volunteers.

Calls, letters, and faxes would pour into state legislators' offices after each alert, according to Bowen's staff. Early in September 1993, Assemblyman John Burton, a Democrat from San Francisco, threatened to amend the bill to require users who downloaded the information for commercial purposes to pay the state royalties. Warren and his coalition members broadcast the fax numbers for Burton and Assembly Speaker Willie Brown on BBSs across the state, and faxes rolled in to both offices by the hundreds. A few days later, the California legislature passed the bill without a single opposing vote. Governor Pete Wilson signed the bill into law October 11, 1993, making California the first state in the country to offer much of its legislative and statutory information free of charge to the public via the Internet.

Warren takes only partial credit for the bill's success. "Basically," he wrote in his e-mail message, "I just had the time, knowledge, and interest in badgering the government into using public technology to become more responsive and open than it had been."

Recalling Roberti

California State Senator David A. Roberti was less than a year away from the end of his three-decade career as one of the state's more powerful politicians when antigun-control activists started a recall campaign against him. Even though the campaign ultimately failed, both sides said the effort to unseat Roberti, who was then the California Senate's president pro tem, was propelled largely by the Internet.

In 1989, after a man armed with an AK-47 killed five children in a Stockton, California, schoolyard, Roberti cosponsored (with then-State Assembly member Mike Roos) a bill in the California legislature that banned assault weapons. The bill passed the legislature with flying colors, making California one of the first states in the country to ban assault weapons, and handing the state chapter of the National Rifle Association one of its biggest legislative defeats ever, according to news reports.

While the ban put Roberti in the public spotlight, it didn't add much to his political stock. When his old district was reapportioned in 1992, Roberti moved to the San Fernando Valley and ran for the seat vacated by a state senator who had pled guilty to federal corruption charges. Roberti spent almost $2 million on his race, but he won a run-off with only 43 percent of the vote against a Republican contender who hadn't spent half as much. Several months later, in February 1993, Russ Howard, a young Los Angeles-area stockbroker and treasurer of Californians Against Corruption, an antigun-control group, began passing around to the group's members a memo detailing the strategy for recalling Roberti.

"Victory is not in winning any particular election.... Our methods make it exceedingly expensive, difficult, and unpleasant for the target to remain in office," the memo read, according to a version of it published eighteen months later in *Harper's* magazine. Roberti, who was rumored to be seeking the Democratic nomination for state treasurer, had stumbled badly in his last election. "The beast is wounded. It's time to go for the kill before he can run [statewide]," the memo concluded.

Around the same time, Jeff Chan, a computer user and gun enthusiast who operated an electronic mailing list called CA-FIREARMS, contacted Howard to volunteer help in publicizing efforts to gather the 20,000 signatures necessary to force a recall. "He said, 'Hey, I'll get the word out,'" Howard told the *California Journal Weekly*. "He said the things he sends out sometimes get to 100,000 people."

Messages about the petition drive began appearing on Chan's mailing list, and groups of gun owners not only in California, but elsewhere across the country, responded. Several groups offered to hold "mailing parties," where volunteers would stuff and send thousands of anti-Roberti flyers to his district. Other mailing list subscribers offered to help collect signatures on the petition and to donate money to the recall campaign.

By February 1994, Californians Against Corruption had gathered 46,000 signatures, more than twice the number needed, and an election was scheduled for April 12. Roberti became the first California state lawmaker since

1914 to face a recall. Both sides in the campaign said the Internet had been a key component of the petition drive's success.

"It's helped us, no question about that," Howard told United Press International in mid-February. Chan's mailing list "evidently does get read. We're getting some dramatic increases in our volunteer base."

"How much more proof do you need?" Roberti asked his supporters in a speech in March. "The use of nationwide computer nets shows these groups are politically very sophisticated and we can't be complacent."

Roberti defeated the recall forces in April, winning 59 percent of the vote. But the fight drained his campaign coffers some $650,000, leaving Roberti less than $100,000 to conduct his campaign for the state treasurer nomination. He lost that nomination in June 1994, and was subsequently appointed to a four-year post on the state Unemployment Insurance Appeals Board.

In contrast, Californians Against Corruption spent less than $100,000 on the recall campaign, according to news reports. In October 1995, however, California's Fair Political Practices Commission filed a 404-count complaint against the group for intentionally violating state campaign rules, including failing to itemize thousands of dollars in contributions from Gun Owners of California and the National Rifle Association. A month later, the commission ordered the group to pay $808,000—the biggest fine for campaign violations in California's history.

How to "De-Foley-ate" Congress

As public interest in the upcoming fall elections began to grow in the summer of 1994, Richard Hartman, a thirty-two-year-old computer software engineer in Spokane, Washington, began to notice a peculiar phenomenon in the discussion groups he frequented on the Internet and on CompuServe. Every time Hartman would post a message complaining about the performance of then-Speaker of the House Thomas S. Foley of Washington, a Democrat who represented Hartman's congressional district, dozens of computer users from across the country would echo his sentiments in anti-Foley messages of their own.

"Whenever he said he was disgruntled with Tom Foley he got more and more responses from people who said Foley was hurting more than just his district, that he was hurting the entire country," said Mary, Hartman's wife.

Most of us would have simply read the postings and clucked our tongues in sympathy. Instead, Richard and Mary Hartman founded "De-Foley-ate Congress," an online political action committee (PAC) whose sole aim was to help remove Foley from office. When Foley lost his race in November, becoming the first Speaker of the House to be defeated in his own district in more than a century, the Hartman's PAC, and the Internet, received some of the credit.

Neither of the Hartmans had ever been involved in a campaign. "We don't know squat about politics," Hartman told the *Washington Times* later that year. But Richard Hartman knew where to find lively online political discussions and he spent a good deal of his spare time corresponding with other politically motivated computer users.

"Someone asked me who my representative was. I told them that Foley was my guy, and I was buried with responses," Hartman told the *Times*. "People were asking, 'What can I do to get rid of that guy?' 'I've got a $100 check—where do I send it?' 'I've got $50, I've got $200—tell me where to spend it.'"

"Lots of individuals were saying 'What can we do to help you?' and 'Where should we send contributions?'" Mary Hartman recalled. "They were primarily disgruntled about the crime bill, about the excessive spending in Congress, and about the fact that Foley had sued the State of Washington over term limits."

Foley himself had beaten a twenty-two-year Republican incumbent when he first won his congressional seat in 1964. As his career progressed in the House, his early devotion to local interests ceded to his increasing role in national politics. Foley was appointed House Democratic Whip in 1981, and he was elected unanimously to the post of House Majority Leader in 1986. Three years later, he became Speaker after Jim Wright, a Democrat from Texas, resigned.

As Congress' popularity with the public ratcheted downward in the wake of the 1991 House Bank and Post Office scandals, however, Foley's reputation was tarnished by association. In 1992, Washington voters adopted a term limits initiative by a vote of fifty-two to forty-eight. The initiative would have applied limits immediately to incumbents had Foley not challenged it in court. He won the lawsuit, but many Washington voters didn't forgive him for filing it.

"The term limits lawsuit was the last straw," Hartman said in a press release about the formation of De-Foley-ate Congress that the National Republican Congressional Committee sent the media in September 1994. "When Washington State voters overwhelmingly approved term limits, Foley went to court and had the vote thrown out. That left no room for doubt. Foley went out of his way to oppose the wishes of his own people, and now they're mad. They want to get rid of him."

Traditionally, angry voters have solicited money for an anti-incumbent campaign by going door-to-door in their neighborhoods and cadging money from the political party that opposes the incumbent. But the De-Foley-ate Congress campaign did its fundraising entirely in cyberspace. The Hartmans posted messages about the PAC's activities in Usenet discussion groups on the Internet and on commercial online services such as America Online and CompuServe.

The messages noted that De-Foley-ate Congress wouldn't give the money it raised to the candidates, but would use the funds instead to run an independent advertising campaign to educate voters about Foley's record. Donations began flowing in after the Hartmans were featured in stories by several major newspapers. Donation amounts ranged from $2 to $200, but $25 was the average, Mary Hartman said. Nonetheless, she was pleased with the results. "We are trying to make this PAC something that the average citizen can donate to in order to help with this effort," she said.

De-Foley-ate Congress also set up an electronic campaign headquarters on the Internet, where computer users could find campaign reports, election updates, a calendar of events, and the address and account number for the campaign fund. As word of the campaign got out across the Net, computer users in neighboring cities would log on to the PAC's files, download De-Foley-ate Congress fliers, and print them from their computer screens, according to news reports.

All told, the Hartmans raised $30,000, which the PAC spent on ads opposing Foley and to defray the cost of printing anti-Foley bumper stickers, pins, T-shirts, and leaflets. Republican George R. Nethercutt Jr. beat Foley in the November election 51 to 49 percent.

Throughout the De-Foley-ate Congress campaign, the Hartmans kept careful notes of their activities. "This is being considered almost a pilot, as a model for the '96 elections," Mary Hartman said. "So we know we're being watched."

Defeating a "Gag Rule on the Grass Roots"

A seminar on "Riding the Information Highway" was one of the most popular events the Christian Coalition, the conservative group headed by televangelist Pat Robertson, offered at its national conference in Washington in September 1994. So many people crowded into the small meeting room in the Washington Hilton that Saturday afternoon that listeners stood two deep along the walls, even behind the speakers' podium. I found a seat only because an older man graciously offered me his.

The speakers, Daniel Becker, an Atlanta software developer and former candidate for Congress, and Jerry Bowyer, a radio talk show host in Pittsburgh who was then treasurer of the coalition's Pennsylvania chapter, explained how computer networks gave grassroots organizers access to the kind of speed-of-light communications that could make the difference between a bill's passage and its defeat when crucial votes were about to occur. Becker urged his listeners to get CompuServe accounts so that they could keep up with Christian Coalition news in the "Town Hall" forum.

Later, in an interview, Bowyer told me that, with a modem and access to the Internet, religious conservatives could essentially "produce their own newspaper" and no longer had to rely on the mainstream press for information on the issues about which they care deeply.

"Electrons work much cheaper than the Teamsters when it comes to delivering newspapers. Information is the point of this thing, anyway," he said.

Less than a month later, the Christian Coalition proved how accurate Bowyer was by using fax machines, phone trees, talk radio, and the Internet to bring down, in less than a week, a lobbying reform bill that many members of Congress had considered a sure thing.

The Lobbying Disclosure Act of 1994 was seen as a political imperative when Sen. Carl Levin, D-Mich., introduced it in the Senate in February 1993. Aimed at dispelling some of the growing public cynicism about Congress, the bill would have overhauled congressional lobbying laws of some four decades' standing by imposing strict new reporting requirements on lobbyists and a virtual ban on gifts to members of Congress from both lobbyists and nonlobbyists. Under the measure, members would not have been allowed to accept free trips, dinners at expensive restaurants, or gifts (such as tickets to sporting events) from lobbyists.

But the bill also included a provision that troubled a number of activists on both sides of the political aisle. It required a paid lobbyist to report "the name, address, and principal place of business of any person or entity other than the client who paid the registrant to lobby on behalf of the client." To many members of special interest organizations, this language could be interpreted to mean that a lobbyist could be forced to reveal the names of anyone who had paid membership dues or donated money to the group the lobbyist represented. This clearly would be a ban on free speech, they argued.

The lobbying disclosure bill's backers insisted their opponents weren't interpreting it correctly. The bill "does not refer to" and thus doesn't require "disclosure or identification of contributors or members of an organization," Levin, the sponsor, told the Associated Press.

And there was no doubt that the bill was popular in a Congress whose approval ratings had sunk dramatically over the past several years. The Senate had passed the bill in May 1993 by a vote of ninety-five to two. When the bill reached the House floor ten months later, it passed easily, 315–110, and was sent to a House-Senate conference committee.

On September 26, 1994, the conference committee filed its report and recommended that the Lobbying Disclosure Act become law. Alarmed that the bill was about to pass, opponents contacted then-House Republican Whip Newt Gingrich of Georgia for help. Gingrich went to the floor of the House two days later to denounce the bill as "a deliberate grassroots gag bill designed to kill precisely the pressure from back home that has been so effective in this Congress."

Meanwhile, a wide variety of special interest groups, from the National Restaurant Association, the American Farm Bureau, and the National Association of Realtors to the National Rifle Association, the Family Research Council, and the Federation of American Scientists began to weigh in on the bill. The American Civil Liberties Union came out against the bill on the grounds that it raised constitutional concerns.

When the conference report came to the House floor for a vote on Thursday, September 29, Rep. George W. Gekas, R-Pa., made a motion to send the conference report back to the conference committee with instructions to delete both the "language referring to religious organizations' lobbying activities," and the requirement that grassroots organizations report the name, address, and place of business of the lobbyists they retain and how much they paid those lobbyists. The House rejected Gekas' motion by a hairsbreadth, 216–205.

The Christian Coalition mobilized its forces. After the September 29 House vote, emergency alerts asking members to phone or fax Congress in opposition to the bill began flying out over the telephone wires to the organization's national fax network, which links almost 1,000 local Christian Coalition chapters. Local chapter leaders fired up their telephone trees, reaching hundreds of Christian Coalition members in a matter of hours.

Robertson broadcast a warning about the imminent passage of the bill on the *700 Club* cable TV program that he hosted, while the telephone number for the U.S. Capitol switchboard flashed at the bottom of the screen. And Ralph Reed, then a rising young star in the Christian Coalition, posted emergency alerts on CompuServe and the Internet.

Faxes, phone calls, and e-mail messages began flooding into Senate offices, tying up switchboards, and clogging electronic in-boxes. In the twenty-four-hour period before the bill reached the Senate on Friday, October 7, almost 250,000 people asked Congress to stop the lobbying disclosure bill. When the bill's supporters tried that day to rally votes to quash a Republican filibuster against it, thirty-six Republicans and ten Democrats voted in favor of the filibuster. The proponents didn't get the two-thirds majority they needed to stop the filibuster, and the lobbying disclosure bill died.

Activists who had backed the bill complained that the opponents had not been completely straightforward about the effect of the bill. "The real underlying concerns that are driving this have to do with the ban on senators being able to get trips and meals and entertainment paid for by lobbyists," said Fred Wertheimer, director of Common Cause, the liberal government watchdog group.

Even Sen. Robert C. Byrd, D-W.Va., the former Senate Majority Leader, said that he believed his constituents' fears about the bill weren't warranted. "Further, I believe that [those fears] are based on a deliberate campaign of misinformation," Byrd told the Associated Press. "However, my constituents sincerely are concerned, and for that reason I voted" against the bill.

Reed read an entirely different message in the defeat of the lobbying disclosure bill. "What it ultimately shows is that an increasingly sophisticated network of technologically proficient grassroots activists is now more effective than big-feet lobbyists wearing Armani suits on Capitol Hill," he was widely quoted as saying.

Winning a Senate Seat in Oregon

Rep. Ron Wyden, D-Ore., wowed the online community in 1995 by cosponsoring, with Rep. C. Christopher Cox, R-Calif., a bill aimed at moderating the effects of the Communications Decency Act, the controversial bill that imposed government controls on information transmitted via computer networks. Even though the Cox/Wyden amendment, which passed the House, was later stricken in a House-Senate conference in favor of harsher language, Wyden steadfastly spoke out against censoring the Net. When Wyden subsequently ran for the seat vacated by Sen. Robert Packwood, R-Ore., Netizens returned the favor.

In November 1995, shortly after Wyden announced that he would run for Packwood's seat, Voters Telecommunications Watch (VTW), a New York-based online advocacy group, submitted a "Technology Pledge Questionnaire" to the five candidates vying in the December 5 primary. The candidates were asked to answer yes or no to the following four questions:

- *Laws regulating indecency are inappropriate for the global online world, where users have a tremendous amount of control over what they see. Do you support parental control, as opposed to laws regulating "indecent speech" as a method of controlling children's access to the Internet?*

- *The electronic dissemination of government information, such as through the THOMAS system [an electronic database of congressional information], has been an overwhelming success. It allows greater access to government information than was ever possible before. Do you support the online dissemination of government information?*
- *The world of electronic commerce has the potential to be an explosive growth force in our economy if it is regulated consistently throughout the United States. Do you support a consistent national policy for online commerce?*
- *Cryptography [the science of encoding and decoding information] is a necessary piece for securing the Global Information Infrastructure. To date, the Clinton Administration has failed to allow the industry to develop, sell, and export competitive products with market-driven cryptography standards. Instead they have proposed schemes such as the Clipper Chip that are driven purely by law-enforcement interests and not by privacy or consumer demands. Do you support the industry in its quest to develop, sell, and export products with market-driven cryptography standards?*

Wyden and Republican Gordon Smith, who faced off in the general election after they won the primary, both answered yes to all four questions.

The Oregon Senate election itself was unusual because it marked the first time in U.S. history that citizens voted entirely by mail for a congressional office. Some 58 percent of all registered Oregon voters returned their ballots in the primary, the highest primary turnout in the state since 1968.

Ballots for the general election were mailed in early January, and 1.2 million Oregon voters—59 percent of the eligible voting population—returned them in time to be counted by the January 30 deadline. Despite fears that voters would lose interest in the campaigns before the three-week voting period ended, the turnout proved to be as high for the special election as it had been for the 1994 general election, when citizens had to go to the polls to vote as usual.

In January, shortly after ballots for the general election arrived in voters' hands, VTW also presented Wyden and Smith with a letter signed by four Oregon-based Internet businesses reiterating the belief that the issues raised in the Technology Pledge Questionnaire were key to the health of Oregon's economy. At the same time, the New York group released an "Oregon Special Election Voters Guide" on the World Wide Web.

The guide, which included independent candidate Karen Shilling as well as Wyden and Smith, presented the candidates' answers to the Technology Pledge, a history of legislative activity related to Internet issues, quotes about regulation of the Internet from a January 5 debate between Wyden and Smith, and an "Internet Candidate Matrix" that looked like this:

INTERNET CANDIDATE MATRIX

Candidate	Stated Support for Internet Issues	Has Voting Record To Back It Up
Ron Wyden (D)	Y	Y
Gordon Smith (R)	Y	N
Karen Shilling (A)	Y	N

VTW cannot urge you strongly enough to vote for the candidate that is most likely to defend the Internet as an open medium. This matrix should make your choice obvious.

Wyden's campaign managers also looked to the Internet for volunteers and financial support. A Web site set up in early January offered press releases and press clippings from the campaign, contact information for the campaign headquarters, an interactive form for potential volunteers to fill out, a biography of Wyden, photos of his family, and a "Wyden Cyber Store" where supporters could buy T-shirts and bumper stickers.

On January 31, 1996, Oregon election officials announced that Wyden had become the state's first Democratic U.S. senator in nearly thirty years, defeating Smith by 17,232 votes, a mere 1 percent of the total. Election officials estimated the mail-in process saved Oregon $1 million in the primary and general elections.

Voters Telecommunications Watch claimed that the online vote contributed to Wyden's slim margin of victory. "Wyden took pains to make his campaign accessible to Internet voters through online appearances, an Internet account that answered voter e-mail promptly, by maintaining an active World Wide Web site, and by being the first candidate in the 1996 election season to answer the Technology Pledge," the group said in a message posted widely to the Internet and on the VTW Web page.

Some observers weren't pleased with the part technology played in the Oregon election. "The day may well come when each of us can turn on a personal computer and file our ballots by e-mail. And 'turnout'—the very word will fall into disuse—will be off the charts, maybe. Maybe, because by then who will care?" Boston Herald editorial page editor Rachelle G. Cohen wrote on February 8, 1996.

It's also reasonable to question whether the online community made as much of an impact on the turnout as did the highly sophisticated polling and tracking operations conducted by the national Republican and Democratic campaign committees.

The Democratic Senatorial Campaign Committee sent a letter from President Clinton to 40,000 households in the Portland area before the final weekend of voting. Each letter was directed specifically to a traditional Democrat whom party strategists had determined had not yet voted.

The National Republican Senatorial Committee (NRSC) also identified Republicans in the state who had not voted. In the final two weeks of balloting, each of these people received six phone calls and three letters from the Smith campaign. "Every night the Smith campaign was able to match up the list of who voted with their targeted direct mail and telemarketing effort," John D. Heubusch, the NRSC executive director, told *National Journal*.

The Wyden campaign Web site made it clear that the Senator-elect was pleased by his online support. "On behalf of the Wyden Campaign I want to thank you for visiting our pages," a note posted by a staff aide the day after the election read. "If you came away with a better understanding of where Ron stands, and what is important, then this small outpost of democracy will have served its purpose. If it made you feel that politics is heading in a more informed direction, that was our intent."

Chapter 3

Handing Out Electronic Fliers

Any sufficiently advanced technology is indistinguishable from magic.

—Arthur C. Clarke

There's more to grassroots activism than getting down-and-dirty in the legislative trenches. No military force can advance farther than its supply and communications lines can reach, and the same goes for a grassroots group waging a policy battle. If you don't have access to the same facts and figures the other side has, or if the members of your team aren't working together and speaking with a unified voice, you're beaten almost before you begin.

Beginning in the late 1980s, Washington-based activists sought to broaden the Net's information supply lines by convincing the federal government to make the massive databases of statistics it had compiled over the years available to the public online at no cost. The task wasn't an easy one because an array of special interests had laid claim to major blocks of this information in one fashion or another. Also, some federal bureaucrats were hesitant to allow Americans access to government data that—the bureaucrats argued—they might misuse or misunderstand. Some activists succeeded in their efforts to expand what they call the "right to know," but others were stymied by powerful political forces.

Communicating data effectively to Net users who are poised to act on it is almost as important to successful electronic organizing as gaining access to information in the first place. Here the activists made much more progress.

When the Washington-based advocacy group OMB Watch established RTKNet, it created the model for an online information center that a wide cross-section of citizens can use, regardless of whether they're punching the keyboard of a state-of-the-art computer workstation or typing on a ten-year-old laptop. The innovative approach to organizing, packaging, and transmitting information that New York City-based Voters Telecommunications Watch took in the early '90s has set the standard for online campaigning. And the work of Internet pioneers Carl Malamud and Kim Alexander illustrates the power of the Internet to deliver government and political information rapidly and easily to the people to whom it belongs—American citizens.

Securing a "Right To Know"

As Barbara Cyrus reached for the front door sometime between 9:15 and 9:30 A.M. the morning of August 12, 1985, she noticed a nasty odor seeping into her house. "I thought maybe it was the cat litter," she told the Associated Press. "But then I opened the door to pick up the paper, and it almost knocked me down."

The "odor" that Cyrus and the more than 3,000 residents of Institute, a small town in West Virginia's Kanawha Valley, smelled was a cloud of chemical vapors that had leaked from a 500-gallon storage tank at a nearby Union Carbide Corp. plant after three gaskets on the tank ruptured. The vapors contained not only dichloromethane, carbon monoxide, carbon dioxide, and sulfur compounds, but also a chemical called aldicarb oxime, which is used to produce a highly toxic pesticide. By the time the cloud dispersed, 142 people had been treated for symptoms ranging from nausea, dizziness, and headaches to severe eye irritation.

At the time of the Institute emergency, accidental chemical releases were occurring across the United States with alarming frequency. From 1980 to 1985, when the Institute accident happened, some 7,000 accidents involving hazardous chemicals had taken place, killing 140 people, and injuring almost 4,700 more.

In 1980, Congress established the Superfund hazardous waste cleanup law to respond to just such events. Eight years later, concerned that residents of communities like Institute, West Virginia, would remain ignorant about dangerous chemicals in their midst, Congress added the Emergency Planning and Community Right-to-Know Act of 1986 to the Superfund law. The new provision, now commonly called EPCRA, requires states to set up local emergency planning committees to evaluate local chemical hazards and plan for chemical accidents.

More important, Congress made it a rule, through EPCRA, that chemical companies have to provide the public with information about chemicals used routinely in their manufacturing processes. EPCRA requires chemical plants to report the existence, as well as the quantity and location, of hazardous chemicals held or used on-site to local and state planning commissions. Along with this requirement, a section of the law requires manufacturing facilities throughout the country to submit annually to the Environmental Protection Agency (EPA) estimates of their releases of specified toxic chemicals to the air, water, and land.

That Section, Number 313, includes this order to the EPA: "The [EPA] Administrator shall establish and maintain in a *computer database* a national toxic chemical inventory based on data submitted to the Administrator under this Section. The Administrator shall make these data *accessible by computer telecommunication* and other means to any person on a cost reimbursable basis." [Italics added.]

No federal law before EPCRA had ever required that government information be made accessible online to the public. Section 313 created a revolution.

Plenty of private companies offered government data in electronic formats in the mid-1980s, just as they do today. But then, as now, access to many of these databases came at a price that could run as high as several hundred dollars per hour of online usage.

Few cash-poor community and local environmental groups could afford fees like this ten years ago, so it would be nice to report that the online access requirement was added to the bill at the urging of forward-thinking activists. But that's not how it happened.

At the time EPCRA was being drafted in the Senate Committee on Environment and Public Works, committee staff member Ronald B. Outen was wrestling with the question of how to resolve longstanding complaints from the environmental community about a perceived lack of test data on toxic chemicals. At a conference at Harvard University's Kennedy School of Government, Outen fell into a lunchtime conversation with Dr. Merle Lefkoff, another conference participant.

"I was talking about the lack of test data," Outen, who is now the vice president of Jellinek, Schwartz & Connolly Inc., a consulting firm in Arlington, Virginia, recalled in an interview. Dr. Lefkoff "listened patiently and said 'You've got it all backwards. The problem isn't that there isn't enough information, but that most of the information is held by government and it's not accessible to people. It's true that a lot more needs to be known, but it's also true that a vast amount of material that would help citizens is buried in EPA databases.' That kind of rocked me back."

Shortly afterward, Outen attended a conference on cross-pollution laws where he watched a presentation on an innovative New Jersey project that collected in one centralized location data on the release of toxic chemicals throughout the state.

"Suddenly it all came together for me," Outen said. "I distinctly remember sitting at my dining room table that night and thinking 'I don't know if we can get this passed, but this little nugget is extremely radical because it fundamentally redefines the relationship between people and government.'" The next day Outen added the sentence making EPCRA data available online.

Ironically, neither the chemical manufacturers nor environmental activists lobbied one way or the other for the online access section. "Because the environmental community didn't see industry focused on that section, and because industry didn't see the environmental community focused on that section, they all ignored it," Gary D. Bass, the executive director of OMB Watch, a nonprofit advocacy group that monitors the activities of the White House Office of Management and Budget, said in an interview.

After EPCRA passed, the EPA cast about for the best way to compile its new database and make it available electronically via telephone lines. The agency held hearings and considered a number of options for establishing the service, including working with a university, a nonprofit organization, or a private company that specialized in providing database services.

Finally, the EPA decided to house the new database at the National Library of Medicine, a division of the Bethesda, Maryland-based National Institutes of Health, the federal government's biomedical research arm. The new database, now called the Toxics Release Inventory, opened June 19, 1989—and immediately ran into trouble with the environmental community. "The relationship between the EPA and the environmental community as a whole was bitter and antagonistic at that time. They were surrounded by an enormous distrust of each other," Bass said.

More important, many environmentalists in the late '80s weren't technology oriented. A dispute between government officials and environmentalists arose during the planning stages for the Toxics Release Inventory over EPA's suggestion that it keep the original data on its own computers and give a copy to the National Library of Medicine for the public to use.

"From the environmental community's perspective that would have made for a secret database. To them there was a real policy question about which data was real data," Bass said.

Debates raged over questions of cost and structure as well. It was suggested that perhaps database users should pay a small fee to cover the cost of providing and maintaining the software that made public access possible. But the environmental community argued that paying for information was nonsensical when it was available for free by filing a Freedom of Information Act request. When the National Library of Medicine (NLM) proposed making the data available in "raw" form only, OMB Watch, and other advocacy groups demanded the agency provide a menu to help users search for the specific information they wanted. A menu, however, would cost as much as $25,000 and the EPA said it didn't have enough money left in its budget to cover that.

Frustration with the proposed structure of the Toxics Release Inventory was running so high in the environmental community that thirty representatives of environmental and advocacy groups met in Chicago in February 1989 to discuss alternative methods of getting electronic access to the data, according to Bass. OMB Watch offered at the meeting to construct a dial-up electronic "bulletin board" that would provide simple digital tools with which computer users could hook up to the National Library of Medicine's system, search the database, and pull down the information they needed. OMB Watch also offered to provide e-mail and conferencing services on the bulletin board, so that the groups that were interested in the toxics release data could have electronic meeting rooms to discuss what they'd found and plan a course of action to deal with it.

The bulletin board, called the Right to Know Network, or, more commonly, RTKNet, began operating at the end of 1989.

Today RTKNet makes ten EPA databases available electronically. They include the Superfund National Priority List of hazardous waste sites, the EPA's emergency response notification system, an inventory of chemical production in the United States, and a guide to EPA lawsuits and administrative actions, among others.

In the early days, government officials warned OMB Watch and its foundation partners that running a database of EPA data would prove too expensive to be worthwhile. The data is too complex for the public to understand, officials warned. At the same time, large information companies complained that the Toxics Release Inventory would compete with their fee-based systems and cut into their profits.

"All the arguments thrown at us about cost and complexity, about how the public would misuse the data, were all de facto proven wrong," Bass said. "The Toxics Release Inventory also became a model for many, many players, because it held out the possibility that all the fears that the business community had about competition weren't valid."

A Database Named EDGAR

Once an idea proves workable on the Internet, it spreads quickly. RTKNet demonstrated that environmentalists would seek out electronic versions of EPA data if they were provided with the tools to do so. Not too long afterward, Carl Malamud, a thirty-four-year-old computer whiz with a public-interest bent, showed how access to digitized information on the securities industry would attract an even broader public.

Malamud made his reputation in Internet circles in 1993 when he began producing a series of weekly interviews with computer experts called "Geek of the Week." Written interviews, based on text-only files,

Figure 3.1 The EDGAR project, Carl Malamud said, was "a textbook case of getting the government to do the right thing."

were nothing new on the Net, but Malamud wasn't interested in producing data that other computer users would have to read. Instead, he used his personal credit cards to buy $40,000 worth of sound equipment and began taping the interviews in digital format. Computer users who had the right software could download the "Geek of the Week" files from the Internet, and play them back through the speakers on their home PCs.

Malamud's audio files became so popular that he founded a non-profit organization called the Internet Multicasting Service in a cluttered office above a restaurant on Capitol Hill and began "broadcasting" other audio events in Washington, like speeches at the National Press Club, via the Internet. Soon, the trendiest home pages on the Web were sporting sound as well as data and video files, and computer networks began to move slowly toward true multimedia status.

At the same time, about ten blocks away from the Internet Multicasting Service office, the Securities and Exchange Commission (SEC) had just given formal approval to an innovative program that it had been developing for almost a decade. In February 1993, the SEC, the federal agency charged with regulating American stock exchanges and providing the investing public with information about the companies that trade there, unveiled an electronic database entitled the Electronic Data Gathering, Analysis, and Retrieval system.

Widely known by its acronym, EDGAR, the database includes millions of pages of key financial information submitted by public companies that must report regularly to the SEC. This data includes annual and quarterly financial reports, proxy statements, and corporate prospectuses—in short, exactly the kind of material that savvy investors rely on to gauge a company's ups and downs and to make informed choices about buying and selling stock.

As the news spread that EDGAR would become operational in late April, a number of potential users, including researchers, advocacy groups, and the American Library Association, began to fear that the new database would be priced out of their league. In the past, the federal government had entered into contracts with large information companies that would pay hundreds of thousands of dollars a year for the right to receive raw data, such as federal court opinions or mortgage loan rates, clean it up so that it was more manageable, and sell it to other financial data brokers. Those companies would in turn repackage it once again and sell it—often with a hefty price tag—to the public.

In May, a group of computer and online companies, including America Online, Institute for Global Communications, and Knowledge Systems, wrote to Rep. Edward J. Markey, D-Mass., who was then chairman of the Telecommunications and Finance Subcommittee of the powerful House Energy and Commerce Committee, asking that the SEC provide online access to individual EDGAR filings free via the Internet. In October 1993, at Markey's urging, the National Science Foundation (NSF) approved a two-year, $600,000-plus grant for a pilot project in which Malamud's Internet Multicasting Service and the New York University's Stern School of Business would put EDGAR online.

EDGAR took off. Within eighteen months, corporate and private investors had requested a total of more than three million documents from the database, at an average rate of more than 17,000 documents a day. The Internet Multicasting/NYU project made the SEC information available to "people who did not have it before: students, public interest groups, senior citizen investment clubs, and many others," Malamud wrote in mid-1995 in a posting to the Internet.

The National Science Foundation grant was set to run out at the end of September 1995, however, and neither Malamud nor NYU wanted to sign up for another round.

Malamud and his partners argued that they had achieved their goal of proving that the public wants access to EDGAR's data and that the Internet is a successful conduit for that information. "We are not interested in continuing the database, taking it commercial, getting additional funding from donors, or getting a government contract [to run it for profit]," Malamud noted in his posting. "We will not be submitting a bill for the $20,600 remaining on our NSF contract because we don't feel the project needs any more work. It is time for the stakeholders in this data to step up to the plate and forge a solution."

As the SEC wavered between contracting with a private company to run EDGAR and operating the database itself, Malamud offered to loan the agency enough computers and software to maintain the entire project in-house. He also offered to train SEC personnel to operate the computers that put EDGAR on the Internet. Altogether, he estimated, the project would cost the SEC no more than $175,000 annually to run.

Malamud's critics claimed, however, that his estimates were far too low, and that the EDGAR project would quickly become just one more waste of taxpayer dollars if the SEC tried to run the database itself. Some of the biggest players in the information industry were also rumored to be vying behind the scenes to take over EDGAR after Malamud and NYU bowed out.

Finally, in August, SEC Chairman Arthur Levitt announced that his agency had decided to make EDGAR available for free on the Internet.

"We've had many creative offers from the private sector to keep EDGAR on the Internet after [the pilot project ends], but all of them would in some way limit the amount of information available, or else attach too many commercial strings," Levitt said. "Taxpayers and shareholders have already paid to compile this information—they should not have to pay again."

The SEC began operating EDGAR on the Web on September 29, 1995. While access to the documents is delayed until twenty-four hours after they've been filed, the site includes a variety of new information, including guides for investors and tips on protecting themselves in the stock market, contact information for state securities regulators, rule filings, compilations of SEC enforcement cases, and speeches by SEC commissioners.

Malamud, who initially feared the information industry would try to get the project killed, was elated at the result. EDGAR, he said in an e-mail message, "is a textbook case of getting the government to do the right thing!"

Sign on the Blinking Line

No massive electronic database stands as a signpost to the contribution Shabbir J. Safdar has made to grassroots organizing on the Net. No foundation or federal agency has funded his work, and he doesn't get regular e-mail messages from the White House. But Safdar, a thirty-two-year-old computer programmer, changed the nature of electronic activism all the same, by making the Net a direct, timely, and incisive political tool for the causes he cares about.

After he founded Voters Telecommunications Watch (VTW), a small cyber-rights watchdog group, in 1994, Safdar invented two tools that are now the standard for Net-based activism: online alerts and electronic petitions. "What I really wanted to do was lobbying," Safdar said when asked why he began VTW. "I've always wanted to have an impact on the process."

Safdar learned political activism during college. Forced by financial difficulties to take a year-and-a-half break from his studies at Purdue University, he went to work in St. Louis, Missouri, for a privacy rights group that was trying to repeal Missouri's sexual misconduct law. After he returned to Purdue, he organized a silent protest against efforts in the Lafayette, Indiana, city council to defeat an ordinance outlawing discrimination on the basis of sexual preference. The ordinance passed soon after the protest took place.

After college Safdar moved to New York to work for Goldman Sachs & Co. He began attending meetings of a civil liberties watchdog group,

Figure 3.2 Pioneering online political activist Shabbir Safdar: "Always be polite. Never threaten. Never lose your cool."

but grew frustrated when the group wouldn't get involved in online organizing. In response, he founded VTW.

Almost immediately, the fledgling group began posting electronic alerts and press releases about such issues as the Clinton Administration's proposal for the Clipper Chip, efforts by former Rep. Maria Cantwell, D-Wash., to enact legislation allowing the export of encrypted software, and a bill backed by the Federal Bureau of Investigation (FBI) that would allow law enforcement agencies to impose wiretaps on computer networks.

In October 1994, VTW released a "Legislative Report Card for the 1994 Congress," an electronic guide that rated Members of Congress on the basis of their votes on the Cantwell bill and on the FBI's "Digital Telephony" bill supporting wiretaps. It was one of the first guides of its kind to appear on the Internet.

Congress didn't get good grades from VTW. Since almost the entire House of Representatives voted for the Digital Telephony bill, every House member started out with a "D." Everyone in the Senate started out with a "D," too, because the Senate had given unanimous consent to the Digital Telephony bill when it came to the floor.

VTW singled out forty-four House members and twenty Senators for individual grades, based on a rating system that added extra points for placing a "hold," or temporary block, on the bill (a procedure available only in the Senate) or for voting against the bill. Rep. John T. Doolittle, R-Calif., for example, so actively opposed the bill that he wound up with an "A," while Rep. Henry J. Hyde, R-Ill., was awarded a "D" for cosponsoring it.

A third of the way into the guide, VTW included a provision that had never made its way into a widely broadcast legislative alert on the Internet. The guide named Rep. Elizabeth Furse, D-Ore., and Rep. Melvin Watt, D-N.C., "Rookies of the Year" for "stating their opposition to the Digital Telephony bill to constituents before the vote."

"Voters Telecomm Watch urges you to support these candidates with campaign contributions and, if you live in their district, your vote," the guide added. For possibly the first time in its short history, the Net became a vehicle for the same sort of voter solicitation that concerned citizens had been conducting in their own precincts and neighborhoods for more than a century.

Safdar's new grassroots organizing tools were put to a much more severe test five months later, when Sen. J. J. Exon, D-Nebr., and Sen. Slade Gorton, R-Wash., introduced the Communications Decency Act of 1995—the "CDA" —which has since become a defining issue for the future of electronic communications in the United States.

The Exon-Gorton bill, S. 314—officially an amendment to the 1934 Communications Act—stated that anyone who "knowingly makes, creates, solicits, and initiates the transmission of any comment, request, suggestion, proposal, image … which is obscene, lewd, lascivious, filthy, or indecent … shall be fined not more than $100,000 or imprisoned not more than two years, or both." The bill was proposed as an addition to massive telecommunications reform legislation then making its way through Congress.

Exon took the position that his proposal simply extended to computer networks the same legal protections against harassing, obscene, and indecent communications that already exist for telephones.

"The whole concept of the information superhighway provides such an exciting possibility for information, education, and broadening the scope of understanding," he said in an interview. "I feel that we have an obligation to make this wonderful new system as safe as possible for young people to travel on."

Regulating pornography on the Internet was becoming a popular issue in state legislatures, too. The Washington state legislature passed a bill in May 1995 prohibiting the electronic transmission of sexual material considered "patently offensive" according to "prevailing standards in the adult community with respect to what is suitable for minors." Then-Gov. Mike Lowry later vetoed the bill, but a number of other states considered similar measures.

The Christian Coalition also took a strong stand in favor of censoring the Internet. The coalition's "Contract With the American Family," released in May 1995, charged that the Internet includes "numerous sites ... where hard-core pornography depicting a variety of explicit sexual acts, even rape scenes and bestiality, are available free and can be accessed with a few clicks of a computer button." There were also news reports that the Christian Coalition had helped compile pictures from pornographic Web sites into a blue briefing book that Exon held when he stood to introduce his bill on the Senate floor.

Online civil liberties groups quickly responded. On February 22—a week after the CDA was introduced—a coalition that included the American Civil Liberties Union and two Washington-based groups, the Electronic Frontier Foundation and the Electronic Privacy Information Center, as well as VTW and the Center for Democracy and Technology (CDT), sent out an electronic alert asking the Net community to urge key members of the Senate to prevent the CDA from being included in Senate telecommunications reform measures and to hold a public hearing on the bill.

Safdar's group became the conduit for information between the coalition and Net users, distributing regular Internet alerts that included a brief overview of the bill and why it mattered to the online community; a list of steps Net users could take to register opposition to the bill; the names, phone numbers, and fax numbers for members of key House and Senate committees; and updates on the status of the measure in both houses of Congress. VTW always tacked on a list of organizations opposed to the Exon amendment, as well as directions to Web sites where computer users could download copies of the bill and analyses by civil liberties groups, at the end of the alerts.

Some alerts also offered sample letters and pointers on how to lobby members in person. "Always be polite. Never threaten. Never lose your cool. Remember we're all taxpayers, so the phrase 'I'm a taxpayer' is meaningless," VTW advised coordinators of state-by-state efforts in an alert midway through the campaign against the amendment.

Most important, VTW attempted, for the first time, to assess the progress of the coalition's online advocacy efforts by collecting responses from the Net community. "Don't forget to drop a note to VTW@VTW.ORG to tell us who you contacted," the alerts urged. "We'll tally the results and feed them back to all participating organizations. It's crucial we have this feedback, even if you just got a form letter, or a 'thank you' to your phone call."

VTW posted its alerts to the more than thirty Usenet discussion groups that focused on politics and civil liberties issues and to dozens of private Net-based mailing lists. Other advocacy groups in the coalition sent the alerts to their thousands of members. Since readers usually forwarded the alerts they received to at least one or two other computer users they knew, between 65,000 and 100,000 people read each message within four days of its posting, Safdar estimated. "The Internet is a really good way to get the word out," he said at the time. "You just couldn't copy this stuff, or fax it to people, fast enough."

Safdar's crowning achievement, however, was the petition drive VTW coordinated for the anti-censorship coalition.

Hands Off! The Net, a small, online anti-censorship group, had organized the first Internet-based political petition in February 1995. This group solicited computerized "signatures" by sending e-mail messages to mailing lists and by posting similar messages to Usenet discussion groups. Any Net user who wanted to "sign" the petition was asked to send an e-mail message to S314-petition@netcom.com, with a line stating his or her online address and full name, and indicating whether he or she was an American citizen.

On March 22, Hands Off! The Net delivered to Sen. Larry Pressler, D-S.Dak., then-chairman of the Senate Committee on Commerce, Science, and Technology, a petition with 107,983 signatures demanding that the committee refuse to add the CDA to the telecommunications reform bill. As impressive as that first petition was, it made little impact on the Commerce Committee because the Committee approved the CDA the next day.

At the beginning of April, Sen. Patrick J. Leahy, D-Vt., introduced, as an alternative to the CDA, a bill that called for the Department of Justice to study the problem of online pornography and decide if additional legislation was necessary to beef up law enforcement efforts. Leahy's bill received a lukewarm response, and a month later, the Center for Democracy and Technology began organizing another petition on the Internet.

Safdar coordinated the members of the advocacy group coalition that CDT had organized to support the petition. The Hands Off! The Net petition had used a technology that made "signing" a clumsy process, he decided, so he made it possible for members of the Net community to add their names to the CDT petition not only through e-mail, but also through an interactive form located at Web sites established by members of the anti-censorship coalition.

Figure 3.3 During the 1995 debate over Internet censorship, Sen. Patrick J. Leahy, D-Vt., holds up the first Net-generated petition to appear on the Senate floor.

The response was so enthusiastic that at one point between 10,000 and 15,000 signatures a week were pouring in to the coalition's Web sites, Safdar recalled. "Eventually we just couldn't hold on to [the petition] any more, so Jonah [Seiger, of CDT] just printed it out and gave it to Leahy," he said. By then, the petition had generated over 112,000 signatures.

When the Senate finally took up the CDA on June 14, 1995, Leahy arrived on the Senate floor bearing the 1,500-page petition. "Every page of this stack of documents that I am holding has dozens and dozens of names from across the Internet," he said, pointing to the petition, as he got up to speak against the bill. "These are people saying yes, [studying the issue first] is the way to do it. Find out how to go after the pornographers, but keep our Internet working."

The Senate passed the CDA by a vote of eighty-four to sixteen. The House approved the Department of Justice study, but when the CDA came up for a vote in the House-Senate conference on the telecommunications reform bill in early December, the House members of the conference committee agreed to accept the Senate's version instead. In a last-ditch effort to persuade the conference committee to change its mind, Safdar organized an "Internet Day of Protest" on December 12. Electronic alerts urged Net users to call Senators on the committee to declare their opposition to the censorship provisions of the telecommunications reform bill. Estimates of the number of calls range from 20,000 to 50,000, based on response messages e-mailed to VTW and other anti-censorship coalition members.

The protest wasn't successful. Both houses of Congress passed the telecommunications reform bill with the CDA intact on February 1, 1996, and President Clinton signed the bill into law seven days later. For forty-eight hours after the signing ceremony, thousands of Net users joined the "Turn Your Web Pages Black" protest—which Safdar also created and organized—changing the colors of their Web pages to stark white lettering on black background to signify their opposition to the new law.

Meanwhile, shortly after the telecommunications reform bill became law, civil liberties and online advocacy groups, and the American Civil Liberties Union filed suit to stop the enforcement of the CDA. After an historic trial in Philadelphia—in which a federal District courtroom was wired to the Internet for the first time—the three judges hearing the case decided on June 12, 1996, that the CDA was unconstitutional. The

Department of Justice filed an appeal of the ruling almost immediately. In December, the U.S. Supreme Court agreed to hear the case. On June 26, 1997, the Supreme Court also rejected the CDA.

The court supported the legislative goal of protecting children from exposure to adult material. But the forty-page ruling, in which seven of the nine Justices concurred, found that the exact provisions of the law also unconstitutionally undermined the free-speech rights of adults protected by the First Amendment.

The court also concluded that broadcast content regulations used to censor obscenity do not automatically apply to the Internet. "The special factors recognized in some of the court's cases as justifying regulation of the broadcast media—the history of extensive government regulation of broadcasting—are not present in cyberspace," Justice John P. Stevens wrote.

Safdar believes the CDT petition played an important part in the development of online organizing. Even thought the petition didn't win the day in Congress, he said, C-SPAN's cameras captured for millions of Americans the image of Leahy carrying the document into the Senate. "The Hands Off! The Net petition was designed to coagulate the Net as a political constituency itself. Our petition was designed to target a specific part of the electorate for a specific reason," he added. "Everybody had in mind, when that second petition went out, that we wanted to see it on the Senate floor, to see somebody wave it around like a tool."

Making the Online Medium Work for Voters

Kim Alexander isn't a geek, and for much of the early '90s she worked alone, with a miniscule bank account, to make voting information available online for California voters who could access the Internet. Today, her California Voter Foundation (CVF) is the template for voter information sites on the Web.

Like Shabbir Safdar, Kim Alexander was a political activist first and an online activist later. Her father ran for the city council of Culver City, California—the small town west of Los Angeles where Alexander was raised—for the first time in 1973. Later he served several terms as the town's mayor. Her mother, a teacher, served as president of the local temple and was a driving force behind the establishment of a youth health center in Culver City. Alexander grew up steeped in politics. One of her fondest memories is of the "election night" parties her family held throughout her childhood. "My sisters and I always sold raffle tickets. It was great fun and always exciting waiting for the returns to come in," she recalled recently. "I think this is probably why I've always been excited about elections and have wanted to participate in the electoral process in some way."

In high school, Alexander got a taste of how it feels to lead the political charge on issues instead of observing it from the sidelines. As a senior, she was elected director of the Pacific Coast region of the B'Nai B'rith Youth Organization (BBYO). Around that time, Nestle, the giant foods conglomerate, was coming under fire for distributing baby formula in Third World countries. Critics charged that mothers who received the baby formula weren't trained to prepare it properly and, as

Figure 3.4 Kim Alexander created the first online voter guide in 1994 with less than $13,000 and a borrowed PC.

a result, their babies weren't getting enough nutrition. Alexander joined the fledgling international boycott of Nestle products, and then took up the cause in her own organization. Eventually she persuaded the 20,000-member U.S. arm of the BBYO to become part of the boycott.

After college at the University of California at Santa Barbara, Alexander volunteered for state Senator Gary Hart's ultimately unsuccessful 1988 campaign for a Santa Barbara congressional seat. Four years later, fresh from an internship in the Washington, D.C., office of Common Cause, the liberal social-policy activist organization, she was hired by Common Cause's California lobbying office in Sacramento. In 1993 she met Jim Warren.

"Jim was the person who really introduced me to the Internet," Alexander recalled. "This new legislator, Debra Bowen, had introduced this bill to put all the state's legislation on the Net. No one thought it would ever get through, but then along comes Jim, with his e-mail and his network of contacts. I was lobbying for the bill at that time for Common Cause, and I witnessed first-hand how Jim was able to overcome the 'powers that be' in the California State Capitol and get this bill passed by activating people through the Internet. It was an incredible learning experience."

Alexander was so inspired by what she learned that when Tony Miller, then acting California Secretary of State, offered her what remained of the California Voter Foundation, she took it without hesitation. Former California Secretary of State March Fong Eu had founded CVF as a nonprofit organization in 1989, as a way to encourage voter education, but it had languished under the administration of nontech-savvy office staffers. Alexander broke the foundation's ties with state government and re-established it as an independent, nonprofit organization. Then in 1994, with the less than $13,000 remaining in CVF's bank account, a borrowed PC, and networking equipment loaned by Pacific Telesis, she created an online voter guide to California statewide races and to the battle for the U.S. Senate between incumbent Democrat Dianne Feinstein and Republican challenger Michael Huffington. At a time when only a small percentage of Californians were online, the first California Online Voter Guide tallied a remarkable 36,000 page views during the five weeks preceding the November election.

The following year Alexander and CVF scored an even more remarkable digital coup. "Late" campaign contributions—those made during the last two weeks before an election—can often turn the tide in a close race by injecting funds for last-minute TV ad blitzes. Voters are usually unaware of the impact "late" contributors have, however, because evidence of the contributions are buried in the mountains of paperwork that pile up in state election offices in the closing days of the election. Determined to find a way around the secrecy of late contributions, Alexander handed a laptop computer to two young staffers on the morning of October 23, 1996, and sent them to the California Secretary of State's office to record all last-minute contributions of $10,000 or more to state candidates and ballot measures. After hours of hunting and pecking figures from financial disclosure forms into the laptop's database, Alexander's staffers returned to CVF's small office and posted the information on the Web. The project, dubbed CVF's "Late Contribution Watch," became an overnight success.

The reason was simple: "late contribution" information wasn't available anywhere else but online at the CVF site. Alexander and her crew also had some juicy tidbits to pass along. For example, the *Wall Street Journal* Interactive edition reported shortly after the "watch" began that a Monday-morning search unearthed $740,000 in contributions over the preceding weekend to twelve Republican campaigns from the campaign committee for then-Gov. Pete Wilson—including $100,000 in last-minute funds to each of two struggling state Senate candidates.

Emboldened by their success, in 1997 Alexander and her staff joined the lobbying effort to convince the California legislature to pass the Online Disclosure Act, a landmark bill requiring state campaigns to disclose their contributions and expenditures in "real time," or as they are officially filed, on the Internet. Jim Warren, who had become one of CVF's first board members, again lent his expertise and network of online-activist contacts to the successful effort.

But CVF was only beginning to gain momentum. In 1998, Alexander and her staff built an online database of statewide campaign contributions and identified the "Top Ten" contributors for almost all of the campaigns in California. By then the CVF site included links to more than 200 Web sites for state campaigns, and hundreds of thousands of Net users were visiting the site.

Today, the CVF site offers Californians not only campaign finance data, contact information, background data and Web URLs for candidates and elected officials in the state, and archives of the Online Voter Guide since 1994 but also maps of California's political districts, a guide to the state legislature, and "tips on how to get involved and get your message out." The foundation stresses that it takes neither partisan stances nor positions on candidates or ballot measures. "Information is power, and improving access to information helps level the playing field between those who have money and those who don't," CVF proclaims on its home page. "Exposing campaign contributions on the Internet—what CVF calls 'digital sunlight'—also helps reduce the influence of money by making its role in politics more transparent. Through our work on the Internet, CVF is helping to shape a political culture that is more responsive, accountable, and accessible to everyone."

Alexander believes accessibility is the byword for everything she does with the California Voter Foundation. Too many political experts fail to recognize just how difficult it is for voters to make informed choices, she said. "Without the Net, [informed choice] is impossible in my opinion. With the Net, we can and are delivering to people basic, nonpartisan information that they need and can trust. That's crucial, and needs to be built for citizens in every political jurisdiction in the country."

Chapter 4

Pressing the Virtual Flesh

I emphasize [the importance of formal lessons in the practice of democracy] so strongly because the world of Internet and telecommunications activism places so little emphasis on training. Wowed by the technology, impressed by our new power to communicate instantly and cheaply with like-minded folks throughout the world, we often neglect to build the larger and more complex skills within which any given technology is simply one piece, one tool, one resource. In short, there's a big difference between forwarding e-mail and building a political movement around your values.

—Philip E. Agre, *The Network Observer*, Vol. 2, No. 9

"Welcome to VoteNote," the headline on the America Online screen announced. The words were a sober burgundy color, the screen background a tasteful buff and blue. A little farther down the screen read: "Click and write e-mail to your members of Congress using preaddressed forms." An aura of gravitas hung about the site.

Of all the technological devices the Internet has brought to modern-day politics, e-mail to Congress is now the most popular. Sites that offer Internet users e-mail links to thousands of federal, state, and local officials are popping up all over the Web. With names like "E-ThePeople" and "The CyberActivist," as well as "VoteNote," these sites offer interactive message forms and e-mail directories that make it quick and easy to send an electronic message to your

Senator, the mayor, or even a local school board official at any time, day or night.

And that's the problem. Web sites like these are often promoted as technological tools that allow "busy but concerned people to get involved in government," as E-ThePeople claims. Certainly e-mail is the key to a number of Internet-based grassroots organizing and political tactics that have proven their worth over the years. But if the aim is to get a message across to elected officials, experts in online organizing say, e-mailing those officials is a waste of energy.

E-mail to Congress: An Electronic "Dead Letter" Box

VoteNote, for example, is a successor to an e-mail-to-the-candidates feature AOL originally launched in its coverage of the 1998 election. Within months more than 50,000 people a day were sending e-mail to Congress when key votes were scheduled, according to Kathleen deLaski, AOL's director of political programming. In January 1999, AOL launched a new online area with databases of Congressional and state information linked to users' ZIP Codes. "We are really trying to create a service for the nonpolitical junkie, to help them conveniently figure out who they're going to vote for," deLaski told *USA Today* at the time.

When Internet users go to sites like VoteNote they're directed to a simple fill-in-the-blanks questionnaire with a space for a one-line subject, a message, and the sender's name, home address, and e-mail address. Most sites require users to provide the latter information; as VoteNote put it, "most legislators only have staff resources to respond to their constituents, and this will help identify you as such."

To send an e-mail to, say, Sen. Patrick Leahy, you click on his name in a directory of Senate e-mail addresses, then type your message, add your contact information, and hit "send." The process is fast, simple, and seemingly precise. Those characteristics attract traffic to the sites, their founders say. So does the growing public impression, encouraged by an enthusiastic news media, that e-mail campaigns are increasingly successful in achieving their goals.

In 1996, for example, there was a rash of reports on how Internet users, convinced that the Federal Communications Commission was about to propose an Internet tax, barraged the agency with more than 200,000 messages in less than a week. The FCC had nothing remotely resembling an Internet tax on the drawing board—the "Net tax" scare resulted from an elaborate hoax—but the flood of messages reportedly shut down the FCC e-mail system and public affairs computers.

After MoveOn.org generated its massive messaging effort to Congress in late 1998, e-mail campaigns began to pop up on computer screens all over Washington. In January 1999, for example, another twelve million e-mails venting public feeling on the President's impeachment poured into the Senate, where the impeachment trial was held. In February of that year, the National Association of Realtors organized a massive e-mail campaign also directed at the Senate, which was considering a proposal to divert obscure real estate transaction fees away from the association's members. Then, the Federal Deposit Insurance Corporation (FDIC) dropped a proposed regulation requiring certain banks to track activity in their customers' accounts after 205,000 e-mails arrived in the agency's electronic inbox in March opposing the regulation on the grounds that it was a government invasion of privacy.

Two months later, in April, the U.S. Forest Service changed its rules on e-mail after a former agency employee-turned-environmental-activist managed to send e-mail to almost all of the 34,000 Forest Service employees. Soon after the activist sent his mailing, another forty groups and individuals active in forest-related causes demanded e-mail addresses for all the agency's employees, too. According to the Associated Press, Forest Service Chief Mike Dombeck finally "decided to become a human filter for all the digital discourse" by requiring that anyone who wanted to send a message to all Forest Service employees first had to send it to him for approval.

Organizers of these campaigns say they're cheaper and more immediate than traditional letter-, fax-, or telegram-based lobbying campaigns. With the Internet, there are no bills for paper, envelopes, or postage when supporters send their messages to Washington. There are no long-distance phone charges or fees for a "phone bank" with operators who manually connect callers with the appropriate Congressional office.

Plus, unlike the paper-based traditional mail, messages sent via e-mail arrive at their destination within a few hours at the most. "Any good office will report to the Senator or representative on a daily basis what the mail is like, and e-mail provides a very accurate accounting daily of public opinion," Lee Verstandig, the Realtor association's vice president for government affairs, told the *Philadelphia Inquirer*.

In the case of the FDIC's "Know Your Customer" proposal to monitor individual bank accounts, citizens were actively encouraged to use e-mail to voice their opinions. For almost three and a half months the agency maintained an area on its Web site that described the proposal and offered an e-mail box for comments, the *New York Times* reported. Each e-mail was printed, tabulated, read by an FDIC lawyer, and summarized in a weekly report. In the past, "the FDIC would receive only a few hundred comments on even the most controversial regulations, and those comments generally came from banking officials," the *Times* reported. The "Know Your Customer" proposal received a total of 257,000 comments—more than 80 percent of them via e-mail—and only about fifty comments favored the proposal.

In reality, however, few e-mail campaigns have been that successful. MoveOn.Org didn't stop the impeachment hearings, the subsequent e-mails to the Senate didn't stop the impeachment vote, and the e-mail campaign directed at the U.S. Forest Service only succeeded in adding another line to Chief Dombeck's job description.

A glitch in the House's centralized servers in mid-December 1998 also sent the House's e-mail software into a "continuous loop," bouncing the flood of messages on impeachment back and forth repeatedly between the central servers and the servers in Members' offices but never delivering the messages. The electronic congestion reached such a level a few weeks later, in fact, that a much-publicized "Billion Byte March" aimed at convincing Congress to establish individual Social Security investment accounts came to a halt because its messages couldn't get through the House servers. At one point before the House voted, for example, Members of Congress were receiving an unprecedented volume of e-mail; almost 1,000 e-mails, faxes, and letters per day flowed into the office of Rep. Billy Tauzin, R-La., while Rep. Bob Ney, R-Ohio—who was widely reported to be undecided about impeachment—received some 7,000 e-mails on the weekend before the vote, the online news service *ZDNet News* reported.

Such floods of e-mail don't accomplish much because Members of Congress and their staffs don't have time to read all the messages, critics say. Rep. Barney Frank, D-Mass., for example, even warns constituents of that problem with this message on his Web site: "To WWW Surfers: I do not maintain an e-mail address. The significant increase in mail volume that would result would place too great a strain on my resources and my staff's ability to keep up with their already heavy workload. However, I will, as always, gladly respond to any question, comment, or inquiry received by letter or phone call. Thank you."

Characteristically, the forthright Rep. Frank may be saying out loud what other Members of Congress are thinking in private. In a December 1998 study that surveyed Congress on the value of constituent e-mail, OMB Watch, a Washington-based advocacy group, found that Congressional offices take personal letters sent through the regular mail most seriously, followed by personal visits and telephone calls. Faxes and e-mail rank "considerably below" personal visits in terms of effectiveness, the study noted, while petitions, form letters via regular mail, and postcard campaigns rank at the bottom.

Members of Congress "are very concerned about being overwhelmed by e-mail," the study concluded. "Precisely because it is so easy and quick to use, it is far more likely that someone will e-mail her or his Member rather than taking the time to write a letter, put it into an envelope, put a stamp on it, and mail it. Many [survey] respondents indicated that this is why they rank e-mail lower than other forms of communication."

Congressional staffers also complain that too often it's difficult to figure out where electronic messages come from. E-mail addresses don't give any indication of the sender's actual geographic location, and that flummoxes members whose traditional practice has been to respond primarily to requests from the people whom they represent.

"What's happening is that with the new software programs today, 16,000 kids at a college can send me a letter with a push of a button," Representative Sam Gejdenson, D-Conn., complained. Gejdenson said he reads his own e-mail and responds to it as much as he can. But, "I don't have the ability to go through all of [it]. As far as I'm concerned, the first people who deserve an answer are the people from my district."

The other great drawback to e-mail campaigns is that they are easy to ignore. When constituents start a letter-writing campaign, and huge brown canvas bags of mail filled with hundreds of letters begin to crowd out the chairs in the cramped reception area of a typical Congressional office, someone on the staff will be forced to pay attention. If constituents organize a phone bank and the office telephones are ringing off the wall, driving the staff crazy, it's hard to argue that the people back home don't care about an issue. But e-mail arrives silently and doesn't take up physical space in the office. And e-mail campaigns are so easy to organize that many Members of Congress don't consider them reliable indicators of public opinion, critics say.

"We have discovered that, while at first e-mail was effective because it hit legislators off guard, what has happened is that so many people have been using it and it is so simple that its value has decreased," Ken Deutsch of Issue Dynamics Inc., a Washington firm that develops an Internet presence for corporations, nonprofit groups, political parties, and candidates, told the *Philadelphia Inquirer*.

This isn't to say that Congress as a whole shuns electronic communications with constituents. Take, for example, the Congressional Internet Caucus, which was established in March 1996 by a handful of House and Senate members and now numbers more than 100 members of both houses. "One of the things our Web page will allow us to do eventually is provide a funnel directly into Congress," then-Rep. Rick A. White, R-Wash., a caucus cofounder, said at the group's inaugural press conference.

Then, too, folks on Capitol Hill tend to love e-mail in one special instance—when it's carrying a message from them to the voters.

Bulk e-mail, which carries hundreds of messages at a time, is fast becoming one of Congress' favorite uses for the Internet, according to a recent Associated Press report.

Since the House Administration Committee amended the franking privilege in February 1999 to include mass e-mails, more and more Members of Congress are discovering that the Internet offers a fast, easy, and cheap way to communicate with their constituents. Each week Rep. Asa Hutchinson, R-Ark., for example, e-mails his legislative schedule and an update on issues to more than 5,000 constituents. House Majority Leader Dick Armey, R-Tex., has over 10,000 names on his bulk e-mail list, the AP reported.

Even the critics predict that, in the future, Congressional offices will learn to accommodate e-mail into their procedures for taking the pulse of the public on the issues. In a 1992 survey by the public relations firm Burson-Marsteller, Congressional offices ranked faxes very low and said that the fax should "only be used in emergencies," the OMB Watch study noted. "Today, faxes are quite common and highly regarded in Congress. Although e-mail is newer than faxes, it already ranks as highly as faxes do as a means of communication. … Thus, it is not unlikely that e-mail will become a highly accepted form of communication."

Action Alerts

In comparison, e-mailing your fellow citizens legislative "action alerts" works wonders because, at heart, people like to gossip. The news doesn't have to be vicious or bad. It just has to be news to the person on the receiving end of the conversation. The Internet magnifies this human tendency to pass on new and interesting information a thousandfold because of the electronic phenomenon known as forwarding. Passing on messages to friends online became a mark of good etiquette early in the Net's history because ARPANet was originally designed to spread information simultaneously to a multitude of locations. By passing messages along to other people, early ARPANet users added to the network's vitality. These days, when one person on one mailing list can forward information to everyone else on the list simply by forwarding a message to the mailing list itself, alerts can reach astounding numbers of people within a very short time.

This power to spread information rapidly in an infinite number of directions makes the Internet a more potent political organizing tool, within a certain segment of the population, than any other. Direct mail marketing takes a week or more to garner a response. Telephone banks, which patch callers through to lawmakers' offices, work only after voters have been notified by some other means to place the call. On the Internet, a voter could conceivably respond via phone, fax, or e-mail within minutes after organizers post their message.

There are good alerts and there are bad alerts. To craft the former, and avoid the latter, include the following:

- *An identifier.* State your organization's full formal name, not a nickname. (Would you know that "VTW" means Voters Telecommunications Watch if you hadn't read the group's full name in previous chapters?) It helps to mention the city in which your group is located, but that's not mandatory.
- *The current date and a "stop" date.* People won't have any idea if you want them to take action today, next week, or next year if you don't tell them what day the alert went out. When legislation is barreling through Congress at a fast clip, some groups even put the time of day on their alerts, but generally this isn't necessary. It is crucial to add the date after which the action you're urging will no longer be effective. Many people check their e-mail only once or twice a week. If they check in on Friday, read the alert you sent on Monday, make a call to the lawmaker's office and discover that the bill went to a vote on Wednesday and it's too late to add their two cents' worth, they're not going to be pleased.
- *Background information on the issue.* When newspaper reporters cover an ongoing event they always restate the central facts in the second or third paragraph of each succeeding story, for the benefit of readers who have just tuned in, as it were. You should pick up that habit. Never assume that everybody who reads your alert knows all the details of the issue just because you've already explained those details in your preceding messages. The restatement doesn't have to be lengthy. A few succinct sentences, telling who, why, and where will suffice.
- *Explicit instructions about the action you wish Net users to take.* The people who read your alerts have varying amounts of political experience. Some have been writing letters to the White House since the day they first picked up a pencil. Some may not have even bothered to vote in years. However, each one of them can contribute an important voice in favor of your issue. Tell them exactly how to do what you want them to do. Give them names, telephone numbers, fax numbers, regular mail addresses, and e-mail addresses. Some activist organizations even include a script telling readers what to say when the lawmaker's receptionist picks up the phone. A lot of civil liberties advocates don't

like that idea because they say it smacks of manipulation, but you can make up your own mind on that score.

- *An address, or addresses, where readers can go for additional information.* Again, provide names, addresses, and phone and fax numbers for all the organizations represented in your alert. The more that people know about your issue, the better advocates they'll be.
- *A description of your organization.* Tell people who you are and what you represent. This makes your information appear trustworthy and gets you a little bit of publicity in the bargain. Always put this notice at the end of the alert because it signifies that your message has come to an end.
- *Include the phrase "post where appropriate."* This suggestion comes from Phil Agre, a professor at the University of California at San Diego who has done extensive research into political use of the Internet. "Do not say 'forward this to everyone you know,'" Agre advises, "so that people aren't encouraged to send your alert to mailing lists where it doesn't belong."

Electronic Petitions

Electronic petitions are different from action alerts because they are a passive activity. An alert calls for each person who reads it to make an immediate response to a specific legislator or group of legislators. Alerts may ask for more than one kind of response, or responses both to the lawmakers and to the petition organizers themselves, or a continuing series of responses, particularly when a proposal is moving in two different chambers. A petition also calls for a response—the reader is asked to "sign" his or her name electronically—but once that response is completed, no other action is necessary.

Petitions also differ from action alerts in that they present a united front instead of individual demands. While an action alert asks voters to say "I care," a petition asks voters to say "We care." Traditionally, political organizers have undertaken petition drives in an attempt to show lawmakers that a large percentage of the community agrees that a particular issue should be decided one way or the other. Electronic petitions should be used for the same purpose.

While petitions can be very effective in demonstrating broad popular support for or opposition to an issue, they're not to be undertaken lightly. Collecting signatures on a paper-based petition is a labor-intensive effort, and collecting electronic "signatures" can be a lot of work, too. Not only does somebody have to write the petition and its accompanying documents, and send it out over the Internet, but somebody also has to collect the signatures, cull those that seem questionable, and organize the rest in a coherent fashion. Printing the petition can also be an arduous task if the response to it has been heavy—the anti-censorship petition delivered to Congress in March 1995 was more than 1,000 pages long.

Finally, a petition works best if it's delivered in person. There's no law against sending a petition to a lawmaker through the mail, of course, but the petition loses a lot of punch with that method of delivery. A group of people arriving at a lawmaker's office to present a petition, with all the fanfare that entails, is much more effective. The goal, after all, is to create the perception that the public is solidly behind the issue the petition addresses.

The principles that apply to action alerts also apply, for the most part, to the documents that announce or accompany a petition: the sponsor or sponsors should be clearly delineated, the date the petition began should be noted, there should be enough background information so that those who sign the petition know exactly what they're supporting, and plenty of contact information should be included. Don't make the petition itself too long, the pros advise. State your position succinctly and forcefully, and then stop.

Unlike an action alert, a petition doesn't physically go anywhere on the Internet. Instead, Net users send their electronic signatures to a collection point via e-mail. Therefore, it's imperative to have some sort of verification system working at the collection site that double-checks each signature as it arrives. Many electronic mailing list programs available now have automatic response capabilities that allow you to send a letter back to each signer, thanking him or her for supporting you and suggesting further action to be taken on the issue. Using this feature isn't simply good manners. If the signature has in fact been forged in some way—if some unauthorized person "signed" the petition with another person's e-mail address—you can be sure the rightful address owner will let you know about it.

Eight Tips for Grassroots Organizing Online

Anyone who wanted to log on to the Internet in its early days had to have a fair amount of technical skill. Not only was access to a mainframe computer a necessity, but also potential users had to be able to work with UNIX, the adaptable but complex computer language that was the lingua franca of the early Net. Few Americans had both of these, and those who did tended to be scientists, engineers, and computer programmers who shared a common outlook on how electronic communications should be conducted.

These early "Netizens" didn't worry about censorship because most people who might have disagreed with them on the question of what material was appropriate for computer transmissions didn't even know how to find a mainframe's "on" switch. They didn't have to fret much over copyright laws—because they had written much of the text being passed around on the Net themselves, or over government restrictions against cryptography, because most of them worked for the government. Back in those days, Netizens made up the rules for life on the Internet as they went along.

This frontier mentality continues to be a part of Net culture, and it's not a wholly bad part. The sense of wonder, the energy, and the belief in technology's promise that the Internet fosters in many people are admirable characteristics. But the defiance of convention that once worked well in cyberspace is no longer the right tactic for rallying supporters to a cause in the twenty-first century. If you want to transmit an effective political message you can't simply throw a plea up on the Internet and expect the public to understand, and act on, it. Successful political mobilization requires careful planning and a clear goal. Here are some suggestions on how to achieve both.

Get Your Facts Straight

"Hello folks," the anonymous e-mail read. "Please read the following carefully if you intend to stay online and continue using e-mail." The message—which spread like wildfire a couple of years ago through thousands of discussion groups and mailing lists—explained that the U.S. Postal Service was lobbying for Bill 602P, which would require Internet Service Providers to pay a five-cent surcharge on every e-mail they delivered. Congressman Tony Schnell "has even suggested a twenty- to forty-dollar-per-month surcharge on all Internet service above and beyond the government's proposed e-mail charges," the message noted. Washington D.C. lawyer Richard Stepp, however, "is working without pay to prevent this legislation from becoming law."

But Bill 602P didn't exist, on Capitol Hill or anywhere else. There is no Tony Schell in Congress, nor a Richard Stepp among the ranks of Washington lawyers. The "modem tax" message was entirely bogus. Wherever it came from—and no one knows that—it created a panic that not only wasted a lot of people's valuable time, but also could have seriously discredited the entire Net community if other alert computer users hadn't checked it out and shot it down.

Don't make the same mistake. Be as factual, honest, and clear as you can possibly be in the messages you send out on the Net. If you don't know the number of the bill you're opposing, find out. If you think a certain lawmaker is willing to publicly back your position, but you're not sure, call his or her office to be certain. If the policy you want to see implemented would help 20 percent of the people in your state, don't say it would help 40 percent just because "40" sounds better than "20." Never fudge or, worse, lie.

Sticking to the facts is just plain common sense, but there are other reasons why you need to do it. First, the Net will find you out if you don't. A major advantage of the Net's many-to-many communications power is that it passes information on to people who know the score as well as to people who don't. Somebody will call your hand, and you certainly don't want that somebody to be your opponent.

More important, when you fudge the facts or create an urban myth like the "modem tax," you hurt everyone else on the Net who's sincerely trying to use the wonders of this new medium to change society for the better.

Plan Before You Post

Know where you're going and what you want to accomplish before you write the first word of your first alert. Nothing makes an organized campaign look less organized, and ultimately less believable, than having to change directions in the middle of the stream.

Think about it. If you found a message in your in-box warning you that a bill had just been introduced in your state legislature to require everyone who uses e-mail to register with the police, you'd be alarmed. If a second message appeared saying the bill would come up for a vote within forty-eight hours and urging you to call or fax your local representative to oppose it, you'd probably fire up the fax program on your computer. If a third message appeared the following day saying, "Gee, we were wrong. That bill was never even introduced," you'd be embarrassed and annoyed. And how likely would you be to pay attention to any other messages from the group that sent you the first three?

This isn't to say that you have to know exactly what will happen to your bill or your policy proposal each step of the way in the rule-making process. Unexpected reversals of fortune occur frequently in politics. But you should have a general idea of where your campaign is going and what roadblocks are likely to be erected along the way. Often a knowledgeable staff member in the office of a lawmaker sympathetic to your cause can warn you of those roadblocks.

Be careful, too, of the technical instructions you give your readers. Sometimes Net users who are sending an e-mail message to their own representative send a copy of the message to every other member of Congress. The end result is little more than spam.

Research, Research, Research!

The Internet is the most powerful data-collecting tool humankind has yet devised. Use it.

It's simply not possible to know too much about the issue that interests you and about the people who will either support it or oppose it. At the very least, you should understand the basics of the legislative process and know who the key players will be on your bill or proposal. You will also be spending your time wisely if you find out which advocacy or trade groups are interested in your issue, and what position they are likely to take on it. One of these groups will inevitably turn out to be your opponent. The more you know about the arguments they might use against your proposal, the better prepared you'll be to defend it.

A decade ago, you would have spent days in a library compiling this information. Nowadays, a truly amazing amount of basic legislative information is available on the Web, courtesy of the thousands of sites interest groups, lawmakers, and legislative entities put up every week.

Don't Flame

No matter how angry the arguments of your opponents make you, you absolutely must keep your temper in check. If you don't, you might hurt your cause, perhaps permanently.

This rule also encompasses those times when you're tempted to question the integrity, honesty, or personal motivations of those who are standing in your way. Negative selling is useless.

Remember that words do hurt, especially when they're being flung around the world at the speed of light, to the e-mail in-boxes of millions of people. And what if your opponents aren't following the "no flames" rule? That's their problem. You are responsible only for the image you and other members of your group present to the public. Think of how much more seriously your messages will be taken if they remain reasoned and polite in the face of electronic rants.

Make Sure Your Message Arrives

Before you spend time and money setting up a Web site, or expanding the one you already have, consider:

- While high-speed "broadband" and wireless services are clearly on the horizon, most Net users these days still log on with modems running in the 24,400- to 56,000-bits-per-second range. Complex Web sites, particularly those encrusted with active graphics, load slowly at these speeds, and the people you want to reach may not want to wait for your message.
- With millions of sites being added to the Web every twenty-four hours, the chances are slim that the people you want to reach will simply stumble upon your site somehow.

In comparison, almost everyone who uses a computer at least once a week has e-mail. "If your objective is advocacy, the Web is not an answer,"

Gary Bass, of OMB Watch, says. "Most community activists don't travel the Web regularly. They will look at their e-mail regularly."

Track Your Progress

Feedback from your supporters is worth its weight in gold. If even a quarter of the Net users who respond to your alerts by contacting lawmakers also send you an e-mail note about the answer they receive, you have an invaluable database on which to build further campaign strategy.

During the campaign against the Exon amendment in Congress, VTW sent out instructions asking everyone who responded to their alerts to let the anti-censorship coalition know what lawmakers and their aides said when constituents complained about Net censorship.

If you're working on a local issue, it is also helpful to keep track electronically of all the myriad bits of information on past elections, voters, precinct profiles, and volunteers that inevitably filter in to a campaign headquarters, virtual or real. Much of this information may not already have been computerized, and you could save yourself hours of flipping through paper files if you've punched it into a database. You may also be doing an enormous favor for online organizers who follow you, since they won't have to go through the same process all over again.

Don't Overdo It

It's possible to dilute your message by sending out too many clarion calls to action, the pros warn. "You can't constantly yank the Net's chain," Shabbir Safdar says. "You have to give [Net users] time to rest and recuperate."

This doesn't mean you should stop sending out alerts if your bill or proposal has reached an impasse in the legislative process. Even the message, "We're still watching and waiting," shows your supporters that you appreciate their efforts and you're working hard to keep them informed of any progress.

On the other hand, a new message in the in-box every day is probably too much, particularly if nothing's happening on the legislative front. You don't want to be accused of cluttering up a discussion list or a mailing list with extraneous information. And if you become the electronic equivalent of the boy who cried "Wolf!," no one will come to your aid when your alerts really matter.

Don't Lose Touch with Reality

Even though thousands of Americans are buying computers and hooking up to the Internet every week, thousands more still don't know a remote login from a remote control. Many local and state lawmakers, as well as some members of Congress, are part of the latter group.

But every lawmaker worth his or her salt knows how to count votes, and it doesn't take much brainpower to realize that the votes that cyberspace represents are still a relatively small part of the total. Maybe someday that will change, but if you're trying to get a bill passed now, "someday" isn't going to be much help.

Smart Web Site Tactics

E-mail campaigns have undeniable strengths. They reach a large number of people in a matter of hours, for example, and there's no better way of mobilizing your supporters to action on an issue when time is of the essence. But Web-based campaigns often can accomplish the one goal that's beyond e-mail campaigns: reaching out to, and educating, a broad audience.

Study after study shows that people who use the Internet do it primarily to get information. Internet users are looking for answers to every imaginable question: What car should I buy? Where's the best restaurant in town? Who's leading in the presidential polls? When does the hockey game start? If they're interested in the issue you're supporting, you can bet they'll go to the Web first for relevant information. If your site is easy to find and easy to understand—if it offers *reliable, clear, direct* information—you'll not only educate people who may know little about your issue but you may also win some new supporters for the cause.

A case in point: the Web site for the "Million Mom March" in favor of stronger gun laws, held on Mother's Day, May 14, 2000. Reportedly the first three actions Donna Dees-Thomases took after she came up with the idea in mid-1999 were to 1) apply for a permit to demonstrate on the National Mall in Washington, D.C.; 2) register "millionmommarch.org";

and 3) find the best Web site designers available. Dees-Thomases originally estimated that about 10,000 people would show up for the march—she was off by about 500,000 heads.

You can't say the Internet alone drew all those people to the Mall, but it exerted a powerful force. The Million Mom March Web site put to use all the Net's strengths by not only telling people about the gun control issue in conversational terms but also by offering them ways to take personal action on the issue. Visitors who wanted to attend the march found maps of Washington and directions to the Mall, as well as an agenda for the day of the event. For out-of-towners, there were lists of hotels, maps of Washington's subway system, airport and train contact information, and directions into the Washington area from the major interstates. Those who wanted merely to express their support for the march could print out bumper stickers, flyers, and paper "buttons" decorated with the event's pink, black, and white logo. Those who wanted to do more were urged to form local "Million Mom March" chapters and charter buses to bring their members to Washington, and given the membership forms, charter information, press packets, logistics instructions, and headquarters contact data they needed to do it—all in files that were easily downloadable from the Internet. Months after the march took place the site was still attracting tens of thousands of visitors each week.

Your Web site can work similar wonders if you want it to do so. All the tips you've just read on successful online organizing apply to Web sites as well as to e-mail, of course. Here are some additional ideas to keep in mind:

Campaign Strategy

Don't make your Web site all of your strategy—make it part of your strategy. An important part, but only a part. This is the single most important thing to remember when you're organizing an Internet-based political campaign, according to the experts. You've got to back up your message face-to-face, talking to the people working with you and your supporters to keep them "in the loop," and to the lawmakers and government officials you want your message to reach, so they'll know the human faces behind the words. If you spend all your time and effort hunched in front of your computer enmeshed in Web design and answering e-mail, you'll be wasting your time.

User Focus

Your site must fit the user's needs. If the people who come to your site looking for information can't find it, they'll never come back. Ask yourself, "What can we offer users?" not "What can users offer us?"

Content, Content, Content

Remember that Internet users look for content first, second, and third. Images and gizmos should be a much lower priority, or your site will seem frivolous. If users want games and funny noises they'll go to a kiddie site.

Always Keep Your Site Updated

The genius of the Internet, as we've seen, is its ability to communicate information instantaneously and without regard to time or geographic boundaries. Because of that, users will come to your site expecting it to have the most recent news and information available for your campaign. If all they find is an action alert for a bill that passed the legislature two months ago, they'll write off your entire effort. Even if nothing's changed on a particular bill or petition, add a note letting your supporters know that you're tracking the situation and will report to them as soon as something new appears.

Be Sure to Register Your Site

Register with all the general-purpose search engines and political portals you can find. The more "eyeballs" you draw to your site, the better. Don't expect to get a lot of clicks just from word of mouth or mouse.

Give Users Things to Do on Your Site

People like to feel that they can be involved in a personal way with an advocacy campaign or with a candidate, so use the interactive nature of the Web to draw them in. Some of the activities that successful sites use are listed below, but don't be confined to this list. Feel free to use your imagination! Invite your visitors to:

- Find resources on the Web
- Sign up to receive action alerts and e-mail updates
- Download a banner for a home page
- Send e-mail to friends to alert them to the site
- Obtain detailed information about legislation
- Identify the visitor's lawmakers via ZIP Code
- Browse campaign finance information
- Follow links to state and local pages
- Download and print bumper stickers, screen savers, posters, buttons, and graphics to create signs and T-shirts
- Discover useful logistical information like hotel location and reservation information for special events
- Get instructions on how to create new chapters in the site visitor's home community
- Study your organization's evaluations of lawmakers' voting records
- Search large databases of information—like a list of campaign donors—online
- Write a letter on the site that can be delivered to Congress as a fax or that can be sent via regular mail

The Internet and Practical Politics

As remarkable as the Internet is, it has limitations. Millions of people now travel on a virtual highway that was originally constructed to carry thousands, and traffic jams are just as much a part of Net life as they are of suburban life in any major metropolis. Signposts are often not clearly marked, and forced detours occur in the most awkward places. Because the Net is constantly evolving, roadmaps become obsolete within months or even weeks. Just getting onto the Net requires an investment of time and money that many Americans don't have.

These limitations also restrict the role the Internet can play in the political arena of the new millennium, some online activists believe. Specifically, they argue that no Net-based campaign can succeed in

Congress without a knowledgeable Washington insider to monitor legislation, talk one-on-one with lawmakers, and signal for immediate action from members of the Net community who live outside the Washington Beltway.

This inside-champion theory has been criticized by activists who say it seeks to perpetuate the traditional power structure in Washington, where lobbyists call the shots and the public is relegated to little more than a supporting role. The Electronic Frontier Foundation (EFF), a major online advocacy group cofounded in 1990 by Grateful Dead lyricist John Perry Barlow and Mitchell Kapor, the genius behind Lotus 1-2-3, closed its Washington headquarters in early 1995 and moved to San Francisco on the grounds that maintaining a Washington "presence" was corrupting the organization's goals. As the Internet evolves, having a lobbyist who can stalk the halls of Congress is no longer a key to influencing public policy, EFF argued.

On the other hand, Taxpayer Assets Project (TAP), an online advocacy group founded by consumer advocate Ralph Nader, began campaigning for legislation to provide privacy safeguards for computerized medical records only because Denise Nagel, an activist who lived in Boston, bombarded the group relentlessly online, TAP founder James Love said.

"If it wasn't for her, we wouldn't be doing anything on this issue," Love said. "She just started sending me e-mail, and faxing me things, and sending me things in the regular mail. Could Denise be a player in the legislative process without an ally in Washington? I say nothing's impossible. It depends on what you're trying to do. And on what you're willing to do."

Most online advocacy experts now agree that personal contact with Members of Congress or federal bureaucrats is a must for a successful lobbying campaign, at least in Washington. Planned Parenthood, for example, now coordinates e-mail campaigns with personal visits to legislators' offices. Seasoned advocates know a message has maximum weight when it's delivered face-to-face, where questions can be answered and points that seem to catch a legislator's attention can be pressed to advantage. Ancillary communications—e-mail, letters, faxes, and phone calls—serve best as a sort of volume-enhancer, a way to prove that multitudes of constituents agree with the arguments being made.

At the very least, be prepared to visit Washington, or your state capital if you're pursuing a local issue, on a regular basis. How regular "regular" is depends on a number of factors, including the immediacy of your issue, the amount of opposition and/or support it generates, and how quickly it progresses from a proposal to debate on the floor of the legislative chamber. You won't know how often you'll need to travel until your campaign gets off the ground.

And if you're planning to supplement the in-person visits with an outpouring of paper-based and electronic communiqués from your far-flung supporters, pay attention to the way most Capitol Hill offices categorize the messages they receive: a letter is better than a fax, and a fax is better than a telephone call, but e-mails rank just slightly above postcards with a printed message and a prepaid stamp. Remember that lawmakers—particularly Members of Congress—value the *effort* their constituents make to send them a message over the actual message itself. Telephone calls aren't effective, Love says, because "not everybody's willing to jump off a legislative ledge based on a couple of phone conversations." The same can be said of e-mail. How willing is an elected representative going to be to jump off the ledge when all you've done is point and click?

Chapter 5

The Dark Side of a New World

The successor to politics will be propaganda. Propaganda, not in the sense of a message or ideology, but as the impact of the whole technology of the times.

—Marshall McLuhan, quoted in *Maclean's* magazine, 1971

On April 20, 1999, Eric Harris, age eighteen, and Dylan Klebold, age seventeen, went on a rampage at Columbine High School, outside Denver. In less than two hours, the two teenagers shot and killed twelve students and a teacher, and then shot themselves. In the wake of this appalling tragedy, the media reported that Harris had allegedly discussed making bombs and committing murder on a Web site he had created on America Online.

It wasn't surprising, then, that on a Friday night a little more than six months later, a teacher monitoring an Internet chat room run by two students from Eastlake High School, outside Seattle, was alarmed to read a message that referred to the coming Monday as "doomsday." The message, written by someone who had logged in to the chat room as "Phantom," warned others online not to come to school on Monday because he planned to kill other students and himself. The teacher notified Eastlake's co-principals and they promptly canceled all classes.

But the threat was just a hoax.

An eighteen-year-old Arizona State University freshman sent the message as a prank, a spokesman for the county sheriff's office said.

The college student, who had never even visited the Pacific Northwest, "is mortified, absolutely mortified, that this happened. It was just a big joke. He apologizes to the community up here," the sheriff's spokesman said, according to the Associated Press.

Only a few months later, the same sort of message went out over the Internet—this time to a student at Columbine High School. Michael Ian Campbell, an eighteen-year-old from Cape Coral, Florida., told the student in an e-mail dated December 15, 1999, that he would "finish what had begun" at Columbine. School officials cancelled classes and closed the school two days before the Christmas vacation, the Associated Press reported. Eventually authorities tracked Campbell to his home with the help of America Online, his Internet service provider. In February 2000, Campbell pled guilty to one felony count of communicating a threat across state lines.

As the Internet spreads into more homes and businesses around the world, and engages more citizens in instantaneous deliberations on the issues of the day, the potential for more than simple electronic mischief grows.

Some Americans believe that the Internet really did contribute to the catastrophe at Columbine. In a *USA Today*/CNN/Gallup poll taken the day after the shootings, 79 percent of the respondents agreed that the incident indicated "there is something seriously wrong in the country today," and more than one third placed "a great deal of blame" for the shootings on the Net. In addition to advocating metal detectors in schools and stricter gun control for teenagers, more than half the survey respondents suggested that a "very effective" way to help stop school violence would be to place more restrictions on the Internet—presumably by passing legislation that would mandate filtering.

The Internet, however, is no different from any other modern means of communication. It can carry bad or wrong or misguided information as easily as it carries correct and honest information. Just as we celebrate the contributions television has made to modern culture—who can forget the pictures of astronaut Neil Armstrong walking on the moon, or of the residents of Berlin tearing down the Wall with sledgehammers—we also rightly bemoan the violence and sheer mind-numbing inanity at the heart of many weekly television programs.

The Internet offers us the same duality. At the same time that the World Wide Web provides community activists who can't afford to travel to Washington access to a wide range of Environmental Protection Agency data on toxic chemicals, it also gives white supremacist groups a soapbox from which to spout their loathsome theories. It moves pornographic images around the world just as quickly as it moves reproductions of newly discovered cave paintings in France or Impressionist masterpieces from the Louvre.

The Net also evens the political playing field for many people by wiping out distinctions based on what they look like, where they live, and how they choose to order their personal lives. But dark corners of prejudice and ill will remain nonetheless.

Some of the other dark corners of this new world pose a danger to the efforts of anyone trying to mobilize public opinion and have an impact on the legislative process through the medium of cyberspace. They are as obvious as the deliberate use of the Net to threaten, harass, and misinform—and as seemingly innocuous as a request for an e-mail address.

The Digital Divide and "Digital Equity"

The Net community is rightfully proud of its inclusiveness. The saying, "Nobody knows you're a dog on the Internet," which celebrates cyberspace's lack of barriers based on arbitrary measures like race, gender, or creed, has been repeated so often that it has become the online equivalent of an old saw.

But the barriers only disappear once people actually reach the Internet. Those who don't have the resources to get wired are shut out just as effectively as if a door had slammed in their faces.

Unfortunately, the door slams most often in the faces of members of poor, rural, black, and Hispanic communities, because they have less ability to access the Net than other communities do. At the end of 1998 over 40 percent of American households owned computers and 25 percent of all households had Internet access, a study by the

U.S. Department of Commerce reported in 2000. Yet black and Hispanic households were only two-fifths as likely as white households to have Internet access, the study, by the National Telecommunications and Information Administration (NTIA), found. And even the poorest households in urban areas were twice as likely to have Internet access as poor households in rural areas.

There's nothing surprising about these figures. Even though computer prices have dropped dramatically—with promotions, to $500 or less—people who are hard-pressed to pay for rent and groceries aren't likely to consider a hard drive and a color monitor part of life's necessities.

But the gap between the "information haves" and the "information have-nots"—the so-called "digital divide"—means a great deal to anyone trying to muster support online for an issue that affects the less affluent. If a grassroots online campaign is to reach these people, it has to do so through simple, direct means that do not tax either their technological or financial resources, experienced activists say.

For a long time, RTKNet, for example, provided an 800-number for its users so that community groups in rural or poor neighborhoods—which are just as likely to need information about toxic chemicals as other neighborhoods—could access the Toxics Release Inventory. "Most of our users are not Internet savvy, let alone Web savvy," Gary Bass said when the database debuted. "Most of them don't have the resources for a Web browser. It would crush their machine. We deal with the 'information have-nots,' you see."

But it's also important for grassroots organizers to recognize that the Digital Divide isn't solely about race or geography. It also concerns the difficulty seniors, physically disabled people, and those with poor reading skills have in using the Internet. It encompasses the gap between young people and unemployed adults who have access to technical training and thus are prepared to seek employment in an increasingly technology-oriented marketplace—and those youngsters and jobless adults who don't have the same opportunities. It even concerns the lack of what some scholars are calling "digital equity," meaning the growing social disparity between those who use the Internet because it offers information that pertains to their lives, and those who find little of themselves or their communities reflected online.

For example, the NTIA study, which is the third in a series that began in 1997, found that, in the space of only one year, the gap in computer ownership between Americans with more education and income and those with less had increased dramatically. Between 1997 and 1998, the study reported, the divide between those at the highest and lowest education levels increased 25 percent, and the divide between those at the highest and lowest income levels grew 29 percent. Around the same time that the NTIA study was released, researchers Donna Hoffman and Thomas Novak of Vanderbilt University reported in an independent survey that affluent black families—those with incomes of $40,000 and up—had all but achieved parity with affluent white families in terms of the number of computers they own and use. Meanwhile, fewer and fewer families making less than $40,000 a year now own computers, Hoffman and Novak found.

So far, computer training centers (CTCs) have become one of the most promising new efforts to build digital equity into the fabric of American society. These community-based organizations, usually established in schools, libraries, and other public locations, provide access to computers and training in how to use them for people who can't afford a computer of their own. With the help of such prominent nonprofit organizations as the National Urban League, CTCs are spreading; currently the League itself plans to set up 114 CTCs throughout the country.

According to the NTIA study, CTCs have become particularly popular among those Americans who have lower incomes and education levels, who are members of minorities, and who are unemployed. As the number of CTCs grows, an increasing number of these people are beginning to use the Internet to search for jobs or take courses. CTC-Net (http://www.ctcnet.org), an umbrella organization of more than 250 affiliated CTCs in the United States and headquartered near Boston, did a survey in 2000 of 817 CTC users at forty-four community sites. About 65 percent of the survey respondents reported taking classes at their CTC to improve their job skills, and, of 446 job seekers, 43 percent had either found a job or were a lot closer to getting one.

Striving for greater "digital equity" will benefit American society not only now but in the future, many concerned policy makers argue.

"A kid entering school now, who uses technology every day for the rest of his life, whether at home or in school, is going to be at a marked advantage to the kid who enters school now and doesn't see the technology until he or she graduates," Larry Irving, the former Assistant Secretary of Commerce and head of NTIA, said in an interview.

"You've heard the saying that it costs more to put a kid in the state pen than in Penn State?" Irving said. "Well, if we don't start giving these kids the ability to go to Penn State, we'll see a lot of them in the state pen, because they won't have the skills to compete in the world of 2007."

Privacy

"CD Software Said to Gather Data on Users," read a startling headline in the *New York Times* on November 1, 1999. According to the *Times* story, RealJukebox software, a free program that some 13.5 million people had downloaded from the Internet in order to play digital music on their computers, was secretly collecting information about its users and reporting the information back to RealNetworks Inc., its Seattle-based maker. Among the data that went to RealNetworks each time a RealJukebox user logged on to the Internet were the song titles and artists on the compact discs the computer user was listening to on his or her PC, the number of songs stored on the user's hard drive, and the type of portable MP3 player (which plays compressed music files from the Internet) the user owned.

Although the comparison is rough, it's fair to say that digital music downloaded from the Internet is to young people in the new millennium what portable radios were to their Baby Boomer parents and grandparents in the '50s—a cheap, immediate, personal window on the vast realm of popular music. Compressed music files, whether electronically captured from the Internet or converted from regular music CDs played on the CD-ROM drive of a computer, can either be stored within the computer or transferred to a wallet-sized portable music player that fits in a coat pocket or backpack. Users can organize play lists of favorite songs in any order they want, turning their PCs into the twenty-first-century equivalent of a personal jukebox.

According to the *Times*' report, however, RealJukebox was extracting valuable data in exchange for opening the door to digital music. When computer users installed the software, they were asked for their e-mail addresses, ZIP Codes, and other personal information. In return, the software assigned each music player a serial number called a Globally

Unique Identifier. When a song was played on the computer, RealJukebox recorded the song title and artist and sent that information along with the user's ID to RealNetworks, without the user's knowledge. The privacy policy on RealNetworks' Web site also did not notify those who downloaded RealJukebox that their music data would be reported to the company.

The day after the *Times*' report, RealNetworks issued a software update that stopped RealJukebox's collection and reporting of personal information. Still, the system alarmed Richard Smith, an Internet security consultant from Brookline, Massachusetts, who discovered the software's data gathering practices. "I saw this as a dangerous trend, where we have our consumer electronic equipment monitoring what we do and reporting back," Smith told the *San Jose Mercury News*. "It's just snooping."

"Data mining," the practice of collecting data about the surfing, buying, and e-mailing habits of Internet users who visit Web sites, has become big business. Sales of Web site analysis and data mining software are expected to climb from $29 million in 1998 to $132 million by 2002, according to International Data Corp. Some estimates even put the value of the data trafficking market far higher, at $70 billion a year or more. More important, data mining software tools are becoming more sophisticated all the time. Even now they can detect where a Web site's visitors came from and what site they click on next, monitor what sections visitors browse and build personal files based on those browsing habits, and keep track of purchasing patterns. According to a report in the magazine *Interactive Week*, for example, Eli Lilly & Co., the pharmaceutical company, has used data mining software to learn more about people who search the Web for data on Prozac, while Paramount Pictures and other Hollywood studios have used it to track which stars are hot—and which are not so hot. It's all part of a trend toward a practice the Internet industry calls "customization," meaning the amassing of information on individuals who frequent a Web site so as to give them exactly what they want in terms of news, information, and advertising each time they visit the site.

Many in the Internet industry say such practices are simply an extension of the sort of data collection that has been going on for decades through nontechnical means. Sun Microsystems Inc.

chairman and CEO Scott McNealy made headlines in mid-1999 when he told reporters at a press conference, "You already have zero privacy—get over it." What McNealy meant, Sun's spokespeople explained, was that Americans give out personal information every day, by reciting their credit card numbers over the telephone when they make catalogue purchases or by writing their drivers' license numbers on the checks they hand the cashier at the grocery store. We willingly give our employers our Social Security numbers—which are direct links to vast amounts of personal information—and we hasten to okay the transfer of our medical records if we fall ill far from home, Sun's representatives also pointed out.

Still, recent incidents show that the power of computer technology is being brought to bear on Americans' personal information in ways they never dreamed. Amazon.com, the giant electronic bookseller, for example, assembled bestseller lists according to what groups of customers at certain corporations or in various cities bought. An ID number discovered embedded in Microsoft's Windows 98 operating system in early 1999, which could be transferred to other documents that a computer user called up from his or her hard drive, was unique enough that privacy advocates charged that any document with the ID affixed could be traced back to the author. A June 1998 survey by the Federal Trade Commission survey found that while 92 percent of Web sites collected personal information, only 14 percent told users why they needed it or what they did with it. The survey also found most Web sites had collected information from children using the sites. Even the federal government's response to its citizens' privacy concerns is largely toothless; a study by the Center for Democracy and Technology in April 1999 found that only a third of federal Web sites publish a link to a privacy policy—an explanation of what information is collected electronically and how it's used—on their home pages, where Net users could find them easily.

Data mining is even spreading into the political realm. As the new century began, a handful of Internet start-ups launched Web sites that aim to cash in on Americans' growing interest in using the Internet to research information about political candidates. All of the companies say they carefully separate personally identifying information from the data they collect and sell. And yet … as privacy advocates point out, what's to keep all that collected data out of the hands of government officials who track extremist groups and other suspected wrongdoers?

These databases could prove too tempting for law enforcement and intelligence agencies to pass up, for example, when they're on the trail of terrorists, David Sobel, general counsel for the Electronic Privacy Information Center, told the *New York Times*. Political Web sites of this ilk could create "some particularly sensitive databases that they would have no control over," Sobel said. "I would assume that users, when they understand the potential ramifications, would be very apprehensive about providing this information."

The key, however, is just how much Internet users really understand the ramifications of sharing their personal data with a Web site operator. When an Internet company talks about "aggregating" information, it means stripping each user's data of such personally identifiable elements as name, street address, phone number, credit card number and Social Security number, and combining the remaining data—about where the user goes within the site, how often he/she visits, which pages he/she visits regularly, etc.—with similarly stripped data from thousands of other visitors to the company's Web site. That mass of information is then sold to third parties such as retailers, advertising firms, and consultants that, in turn, slice-'n-dice it to develop profiles of surfing habits that can be pinpointed down to a single ZIP Code.

It's important to remember, however, that all those stripped-out personal details can be retained in the databases the Web site owner maintains. And any Internet user who has clicked on the site can be identified as long as those details remain in the company's electronic files. Unless the company is willing to make a commitment not to provide to third parties any form of the personal information it collects, the possibility always exists that, somewhere down the road, data that describes in detail who visited the company's site, what they read and saw, and—in the case of the "political information" Web sites—how they feel about sensitive social, legal, and moral issues will be sold to total strangers.

What should you do to protect yourself from that possibility? No tactic is foolproof, and the sad fact is that data-mining tools have even now become so sophisticated that all they need to track any Internet user are the user's ZIP Code and the last few digits of the user's credit card number. But you should always read the privacy policy on a Web site you visit before handing over your personal information. Consider trying another Web site if you're asked for too much personal information. If you decide to stay with the site you're on, try to give up as little identifying information as possible. And think twice—three times, if necessary—before waxing eloquent about your personal beliefs on any Web site that seems a little overeager to draw that information out of you. If you don't exercise caution about revealing your data and opinions on the Internet, be assured that no one else will.

Propaganda

While NATO planes were bombing Serb-held towns during the 1999 conflict in Yugoslavia, another air war was taking place in the virtual ether of cyberspace.

Almost from the start of the hostilities, NATO used its Web site aggressively to make a case for bombing Serbian leader Slobodan Milosevic's strongholds. The site provided not only press releases and transcripts of NATO officials' speeches, but also video footage of the NATO air strikes. The video proved so popular that in the first week after the bombing in Yugoslavia began, hits on the NATO site jumped from 30,000 a day to almost 90,000, according to the *New York Times*.

The Western allies weren't the only technically savvy players in this game, however. Only a few weeks after the NATO site began offering the air strike videos, Serbian hackers disabled the site via a "ping attack"—a hacker's gambit that overloads the server for a Web site with more Internet-generated electronic queries than it can handle. The site was knocked out all of one day and parts of the following three days, until the NATO Web experts could install a filter to stem the tide of the "pings."

The deliberate misuse of a popular communications medium to spread propaganda is an old tactic in wartime. Think of Frank Capra's film series, *Why We Fight*, at the beginning of World War II, or the seductive voice of Tokyo Rose on radio broadcasts throughout the Pacific theatre several years later. Or, go back in U.S. history to the "yellow journalism" of the Hearst newspapers that launched the Spanish-American War, or the patriotic songs promising fame and glory—but certainly not an ignominious death—to young men from both the North and the South who marched off to the battlefields of the Civil War.

With the Internet, however, propaganda can be spread farther, faster, and with a potentially more devastating impact than ever before.

Take an incident that occurred during the 1999 mayoral race in Philadelphia as an example. In late February, political reporters for the city's leading newspapers received e-mails urging them to click on http://www.white99.com, which the e-mails identified as the official site of Democratic mayoral candidate John White Jr. The site certainly looked official—it was adorned with photos from White's press kit—but it gave prominence to a disturbing quote from White that had appeared in the local Spanish-language newspaper *al Dia*. According to *Wired News*, which reported the incident, the quote, translated into English and repeated in bold letters all over the site, read: "The black and the brown, if we unite, we're going to control this city." Both White and his opponent, state representative Dwight Evans, are black.

White disavowed the site, which was registered to Brock Landers, the name of a porno star in the movie *Boogie Nights*, and listed at the address of Robert J. Richman, age twenty-three, *Wired* reported. A few weeks later, news reports revealed that Richman was a friend of David Sirota, also twenty-three, a Web designer and deputy campaign manager for Evans. Sirota eventually lost his job.

Even national political campaigns, with their huge war chests and phalanxes of aides and advisors, aren't immune from the sting of Internet-based dirty tricks. In 1999, the exploratory committee for George W. Bush filed a complaint with the Federal Election Commission (FEC) over http://www.gwbush.com, a Web site that directly criticized the then-governor of Texas, raised questions about his past, and urged his defeat if he ran for President. The exploratory committee's complaint asked the FEC to force thirty-year-old Zach Exley, the owner of the site's domain name, to abide by FEC rules by posting a disclaimer through which he identified himself, by filing officially for himself and the site's creators as a political action committee (PAC) with the Commission, and by making public how much had been spent to build the site. "The confusion [generated by the gwbush.com site] had been so strong that reporters frequently confused the unofficial site with the official site," according to the *New York Times*.

The gwbush.com site wasn't the only Web site to appear early in the campaign season criticizing high-profile potential candidates. HillaryNo.com, a site that opened in 1999 under the sponsorship of a group that backed New York City mayor Rudolph Guiliani, displayed a photo of former first lady Hillary Rodham Clinton with her thumbs up and the headline, "U.S. Senate: For Proven Leaders, Not a Proving Ground." In February 2000, Clinton officially became the Democratic candidate for the seat Sen. Daniel Patrick Moynihan of New York had announced he would vacate. Guiliani was the Republican candidate for the post.

HillaryNo.com didn't mince words about its target. "With no governmental experience, never elected to any public office, her failed health care experiment under her belt, Mrs. Clinton now wants to be part of the Senate as we head into the next millennium," the site said. Unlike gwbush.com, however, HillaryNo.com included a disclaimer notifying Web users that the "Friends of Guiliani" had paid for the site. Also unlike the anti-Bush site, the anti-Hillary site didn't suggest that voters should cast their ballots for or against Clinton—a fact that exempted it from FEC oversight under rules the Commission's lawyers had devised in late 1998.

Clinton went on to win the New York Senate seat, and Governor Bush became President Bush. In April 2000, the FEC quietly dismissed the Bush campaign complaint, saying it wasn't worth the expenditure of Commission resources. Commission observers suggested the decision stemmed from the FEC's reluctance to make rules that could stifle the creative development of the Web during the 2000 Presidential campaign.

The Commission was also mindful of the criticism that its earlier ruling engendered, observers said. When Leo Smith of Suffield, Connecticut, erected a Web site in 1998 endorsing Charlotte Koskoff, a Democrat running for Congress, and advocating the defeat of Koskoff's opponent, Rep. Nancy Johnson, the incumbent Republican, the FEC concluded that Smith's site was a political advertisement. As a political ad, the site had to disclose the name of its creator, report its expenditures, and indicate whether the candidate had authorized the opinions expressed on the site. Smith was even told that the cost of his computer would be considered a campaign expenditure.

Critics assaulted the ruling almost immediately, saying that it stifled political expression by forcing individual citizens to hire lawyers and accountants to fill out arcane Commission paperwork. Once those fees begin to mount up, the critics said, the Internet in essence shifts from being a forum where average citizens can convey opinions quickly and cheaply, to being another high-priced communications medium open only to the wealthy and the powerful.

However, there's a dark side even to the quick, easy communication the Internet offers. In February 1999, for example, Kingman Quon, a twenty-two-year-old resident of Los Angeles, pled guilty to charges of sending hate e-mail to more than seventy people of Hispanic descent, including forty-two Latino professors at the California State University at Los Angeles and twenty-five Latino students at the Massachusetts Institute of Technology, as well as individuals at Xerox, the Texas Hispanic Journal, Indiana University, the Internal Revenue Service, and a NASA research center. According to the *Los Angeles Times*, Quon's attorney, Joseph Gibbons Jr., explained his client's behavior by saying, "He just snapped. He was a high-achiever student ... and he thought others were getting advantages that he wasn't. So he vented. He didn't mean to harm anyone. He wishes he could take it all back." Three months later, someone who was logged on to a computer at Stanford University sent racist e-mail to 25,000 people on campus accusing the university of giving nonwhites preference in university housing. Stanford has a housing shortage, and the week before 1,300 students had failed to win spaces in the housing lottery, an Associated Press story reported. The sender of the e-mail has yet to be identified.

These incidents stand as a chilling reminder of the power of the Internet to reach even sophisticated computer users on a gut level and provoke an emotional reaction unjustified by reality.

This power can be particularly dangerous in the context of Net-based political discussions. Politics is by its definition the arena where a nation debates the issues central to the daily lives of its people. Controlling crime, providing medical care for the sick, protecting our children, defending our borders—these are all matters in which we each hold a stake and about which we care deeply.

Our grandparents had time to digest and analyze an inflammatory stump speech or an artfully crafted bit of disinformation. The telegraph was the fastest way to transmit information at the turn of the century, and even emergency messages could take hours to reach their destination. Radio and, later, television shortened the transit time between the source of a misleading statement and its audience, but both of these media are one-way channels. You can't respond within seconds to a radio ad or a television documentary—not yet, anyway.

The Internet is not only instantaneous, but also interactive. The whole point of an action alert is to motivate an online reader to do something immediately to influence the course of policy or legislation. When the message has been carefully honed and directed to precisely the audience that cares enough about it to act quickly, the result—as we've seen—can be an outpouring of hundreds of thousands of calls, faxes, and e-mail pleas practically overnight.

Read a political mailing list or Usenet discussion group long enough, and you understand how prevalent mental shortcuts are in some corners of the Net. There's much to be said for the discarding of "traditional media filters" like newspapers and television news organizations in cyberspace. But with the disappearance of information gatekeepers, Net users must learn to apply their own individual filters for falsehood and manipulation.

The failure to guard against propaganda on the Net could do far more than clog a few newsgroups and mailing lists with flame wars between far-left and far-right nut cases. As experienced online activists and political consultants well know, Richard Nixon beat Hubert Humphrey in 1968 by less than 500,000 votes, or little more than one vote per precinct. If the Net can muster 250,000 signatures on an online petition now, on an issue that has a very narrow appeal, the day will come when the Net could swing a nationwide election. It's incumbent on any online activist to make sure that power is used in the service of truth.

Chapter 6

Voting Booths for the Millennium

At some point in the future we will review the candidates' positions, get answers on the issues, look at endorsers, check the news, mark a sample ballot as we go, change our minds a few times, check what we've done, and print it out and take it to the polls ... or upload it.

—Tracy Westen, then-president of the Center for Governmental Studies, a nonprofit organization devoted to increasing voter participation, in *Wired News*, November 2, 1999

Marc Strassman first started trying to get an initiative on electronic voting on the California state ballot in December 1995. Back then, California voters were already using IBM punch cards to cast their ballots, so Strassman decided voting online was the logical next step. "It's not like computers aren't used in voting now," Strassman, who went on to found an organization he calls "Campaign for Digital Democracy," told me all those years ago. "I figure, 'Let's just take the power of this technology and move it into the political arena.'"

Around the same time that Strassman began his campaign, a splinter political group in Canada, the Democratech Party of British Columbia, became the first such organization in North America to advocate allowing citizens to run their government via an electronic voting system. "With modern, instantaneous communications, the people can directly make their own decisions, relegating politicians to the scrap heap of history," the party announced.

Americans may not be quite ready to relegate their lawmakers to the scrap heap (well, not all of them), but electronic voting is becoming a less fantastic proposition by the day.

Voter turnout is dropping in the United States at a catastrophic rate. Almost five million Americans didn't vote in 1996 because they were "too busy," the U.S. Census Bureau has reported. In November 1998, only one-third of the eligible voters in this country took the time to cast their ballots—a fifty-year low. The United States now ranks at or near the bottom of world democracies in terms of voter participation.

As voter turnout drops, special interest groups that can mobilize thousands of voters and get them to the polls have greater leverage in the political process than ever before. When citizens who are not a part of a special interest group vote, and subsequently see their votes overwhelmed by an outpouring of well-disciplined opposition, the apathy meter inches even higher.

Voting, fundraising, polling, and registering to vote via the Internet strike some knowledgeable observers of American politics as potentially dangerous. "What about the possibility of widespread fraud?" they ask. Whatever happened to the principle that a democracy requires citizen representatives who will hash out problems face-to-face, rather than via a beeping electronic screen? But other thoughtful political analysts—whatever their misgivings—have begun to experiment in earnest with electronic tools for the electorate. These tools may be our best, and last, hope to ratchet voter participation in American politics to a healthier level.

The History of Online Voting

In mid-1993, the Voting by Phone Foundation, a local advocacy group in Boulder, Colorado, began a campaign to get an initiative for an electronic voting system on the city ballot. The system the foundation proposed worked much like automatic voice mail: After voters chose a password, a computer would assign them random identification numbers and check off their names on the voting rolls so they couldn't vote by a traditional paper ballot. On Election Day, voters would call a toll-free number, tap in their ID numbers, and listen to a digitized voice present the ballot choices. After each voter would record his or her choice, the computer would release an individual confirmation number. Voters would check their identification numbers against a list published in the local newspaper the next morning to make sure their votes had been recorded. The Voting by Phone Foundation's initiative wasn't successful—when it was finally placed on the ballot in 1995, Boulder's voters rejected it 59 to 41 percent. But less than five years later, proposals for e-voting were receiving serious attention in other parts of the country.

In California, for example, Secretary of State Bill Jones convened a task force in March 1999 to study online voting and make recommendations to the state legislature on the issue. Bills to initiate online voting studies were also introduced in 2000 in both Minnesota and Washington state—which was also the site of an online voting test, as were California, Iowa, and Virginia. Florida had also planned an online voting test, but questions of voter fraud in the Miami area demanded more attention and resources, officials said. Arizona Democrats were planning to offer Internet voting as a supplement to regular balloting for their March 11 presidential primary, while the Idaho State Democratic Party was exploring the possibility of offering Internet voting as part of its March 4 presidential caucuses. The Department of Defense allowed the overseas residents of certain counties in Florida, South Carolina, Texas, and Utah to vote online in 2000 in a pilot program that became the most extensive real-world test yet of whether technology and participatory democracy can mix successfully.

The Defense Department test was limited to only fifty voters from each of the five states, but it has a huge potential audience. The Federal Voting Assistance Program (FVAP), which funded the test and designed guidelines for it, provides voting help and information for the approximately six million Americans, both military and civilian, who live overseas and are eligible to cast absentee ballots. During the test, selected voters filed their ballots via computers provided by the FVAP and equipped with specialized encryption technology the agency developed. On the receiving end, local election officials in each of the five states used special technology to unscramble the ballots and tabulate them. In its test run, the system worked "flawlessly," Polli Brunelli, the FVAP director told American Forces Press Service. Military personnel who participated in the online voting process had little trouble—one voter even called it a "snap."

If voting preferences in Piedmont, California, or Mason County, Washington, are any indication, the Defense Department may have a winner on its hands. On March 2, 1999, for example, Piedmont, a suburb of San Francisco, held a computer-based election that generated final results only twenty-nine minutes after the polls closed. The Piedmont election didn't involve online voting per se—participants inserted Smartcards containing ballot information into computers and made their choices by touching the buttons that popped up on the screen—but it attracted more than 7,600 voters. The Mason County election, held almost two months later, allowed voters to cast their ballots through a Web site hosted by VoteHere.net, a Kirkland, Washington, company developing Internet-based voting systems. While Mason County's voters had the option of voting the traditional way at the polls, some 560 voters chose to weigh in via cyberspace on several questions concerning local school policy. A final question on the ballot asked, "If available in your area, would you use the Internet to vote?" The answer, by a four to one margin, was yes.

The California task force on online voting—the first state panel in the nation to study the issue—might have gotten underway even earlier if politics hadn't intervened. In 1997, the California legislature passed a bill calling for an official state study on online voting. Then-Governor Pete Wilson vetoed the bill, however, on the grounds that e-voting would become a magnet for fraud and vote tampering. Two years later Jones reportedly felt so strongly about the potential of online voting that he convened the task force on his own initiative. "Technology and people's expectations are going to force us to deal with these issues," he told the group's two dozen members at the first meeting, according to the *New York Times*. "The rest of the country expects California to lead on this."

Regardless of who "leads," online voting would address a number of ills that plague traditional voting systems, its supporters say. Most important, e-voting would cut the cost of administering elections dramatically. In 1995, for example, Boulder spent approximately $2 per vote on its local elections. The Voting by Phone Foundation estimated, however, that its phone-based voting system would cost only seventy-five cents per vote the first time it was used, and proportionately less each subsequent time as the city amortized its installation costs. More recently, the traditional methods of absentee voting have been estimated to cost over $5 for each vote processed. In comparison, Tim Draper, a Silicon Valley businessman, spent several months and nearly $1 million to place a school-voucher initiative on the California ballot in 2000. If registered voters' signatures could have been gathered through the Internet, the measure might have been placed on the ballot in days at a cost of only a few hundred dollars, the *San Diego Union-Tribune* reported.

Supporters of online voting point to other pluses of the system. Voting via the Internet would help reduce voter fraud by reducing the number of absentee ballots, which are often the major source of falsified votes, they say. It could also help ease long lines and the wait for an open ballot box that voters regularly face at their neighborhood polling places. For example, a proposal for online voting that was considered—but rejected—for the Louisiana Republican party primary in early 2000 would have allowed voters to cast their ballots from computers set up in the homes of several hundred party volunteers throughout the state. In comparison, the Louisiana GOP had made only forty-two ballot sites available for the 20,000 party regulars who had participated in the 1996 caucuses.

E-voting also has the potential to change voter turnout rates dramatically, supporters argue. "While it's easy to lay the blame for poor voter turnout on an uninterested electorate, or perhaps the politics of meanness, or television, one simple truth is that the act of voting is antiquated, inconvenient, and just too hard," Louis V. Gerstner, chairman and chief executive officer of International Business Machines Corp., wrote in *USA Today* in November 1998. "We either improve convenience or resign ourselves to the status quo. I don't believe the latter choice is acceptable—not when the technology exists to allow us to cast a ballot over the Internet from the comfort of our home, or with the convenience of an ATM-like kiosk at work or at a traditional polling location."

But e-voting has its detractors as well. Many of them point out that even now many Americans don't use the Internet. "I find that people who say, 'Oh, everybody has a computer, everybody's on the Internet,' are overlooking a huge portion of our population that is not," Boulder Mayor Leslie L. Durgin said during her city's debates over the Voting by Phone Foundation initiative.

Other opponents note that a host of technical obstacles—including faulty server connections, outdated local equipment, and the potential for system-wide crashes—make online voting an iffy proposition at this point in time. In a thirty-page report released in August 1999, the Voting Integrity Project, a nonprofit, nonpartisan group that tracks voter fraud cases, cited a recent hacking of the U.S. Senate's Web site. Hackers who diverted the Senate's Web visitors to a parody site could do the same to online voters, the report warned. "The frightening thing is that voters would not necessarily be aware their votes were not being legitimately cast," the report said. "Once diverted to such a counterfeit site, their voting transaction could be captured and used to log votes for the thieves' candidates of choice on the real election site, quite possibly without detection."

Even when online voting is successful, it can be very expensive. The cost of designing software and installing computers for, and analyzing the results of, the Defense Department's Internet-based voting system ran more than $6 million, according to the Center for Public Integrity—meaning that the eighty-four votes cast cost $74,000 each.

Also, making it easier for people to vote doesn't guarantee that they'll take advantage of the opportunity, David Mason, director of congressional studies at the Heritage Foundation, a conservative Washington think tank, said. "In the days when people had to walk on foot and ride on horseback to vote we had a higher turnout than today," he said.

He also fears that citizens who don't engage in face-to-face debate on the issues may lose the sense of personal responsibility that keeps a democracy alive. "When you vote, you come to the same place as other people, you wait in line with other people, you see candidates standing outside the polling area," he said. "The problems of people feeling alienated could be exacerbated by relying entirely on the computer or the phone, simply because the distance between what the voters do and the final action of the government is that much greater."

Linda Valenty, a professor of political science at San Jose State University and a member of the California online voting task force, issues a similar warning. "The potential criticism is, if you simply want to increase voter turnout, have a twenty-four-hour voting day," Valenty told the *New York Times*. "If you want to increase voter turnout, fine people for not voting, as they do in Australia."

Fines might spur older voters to the polls, but they're likely to have little or no effect on younger voters—the group election officials are desperate to attract. In 1998, some two million eligible voters between eighteen and twenty-four didn't vote. And a paltry 15 percent of the same age group voted in the 1996 presidential election, said Iowa Secretary of State Chet Culver, who spearheaded his state's pilot program on e-voting. "We have historical lows with voter participation and turnout—especially among young people," Culver told *Wired News*. "They feel intimidated by the process or uncomfortable with the procedure, and this will hopefully make it easier for young people to vote."

Younger voters certainly seem to respond to voting via the Internet. When Votehere.Net held a mock Internet election at fifteen high schools in the Charlottesville, Virginia, area in October 1999, more than 60 percent of the 7,000 "registered voters" turned out. In comparison, voter turnout in the Mason County, Washington, special election only six months before had been only 9.6 percent.

Campaign strategists can't afford to ignore such numbers, particularly when the trend is toward razor-thin margins in national races. Online voting may not become an Election Day staple in this country for a decade or more, but it's not an idea that's going to go away.

Online Fundraising

Jean Elliott Brown of West Palm Beach, Florida, would never have run for political office if it weren't for the Internet.

A former public relations director for several large companies and the founder of her own PR firm, Brown had had little to do with politics until October 1998, when she signed a MoveOn petition and volunteered to deliver it at completion to Rep. Mark Foley, the Republican who represented her home congressional district. When Foley voted for two of the four articles of impeachment against President Clinton, the *Palm Beach Post* interviewed Brown about her activities for MoveOn. The newspaper story generated calls from throughout the district urging Brown to run for Foley's seat, and she did.

Within weeks, Brown was receiving national attention. Singer/songwriter Jimmy Buffett joined her campaign steering committee and a crew from *Good Morning America* did a feature story on her, the *New York Times* reported. Less than six months later, Brown had raised more than $140,000. Almost one-third of those funds came from donations collected by MoveOn, which set up a mechanism on its Web site for Internet users to send money to Democrats in four congressional races against Republicans who had voted for impeachment. In a fifth race, MoveOn supported Democrat Rush Holt of New Jersey—who had voted no on impeachment—against a well-financed Republican challenger.

Most of the Internet-based donations were in the $10-$50 range, and many came from outside Brown's district, a fact she cheerfully acknowledged on her Web site. "It is in everyone's interest to take back the U.S. House in 2000," one of the answers to the site's FAQ, or "Frequently Asked Questions," noted. "Remember, 95 percent of the votes a Representative makes are not strictly for the district. He or she is voting on issues that affect not only all Americans, but people around the world."

Brown's willingness to accept donations from voters outside her district might have been somewhat unusual, but her effort to raise money via the Internet clearly was not. Online fundraising holds so much promise for attracting thousands of so-called small donors—those ordinary folk who don't belong to powerful PACs or who can't make the $1,000 donation allowed by law—that some political strategists believe it could revolutionize campaigns of the future.

Some of the biggest campaign headlines in recent years have come from the successes national candidates have had raising money via the Internet. Sen. Bill Bradley raised more than $1.2 million by the end of 1999 in his bid for the Democratic presidential nomination. Just a few months later, Sen. John McCain startled traditionalists in the political world by raising over $3 million through his Web site after he won the New Hampshire Republican primary. Even though both Bradley and McCain were eventually defeated, experts say their online fundraising feats may have changed Internet politics for good.

Gathering funds on the Internet for political purposes has a longer history, in Net terms, than many people realize. The first online PAC, or political action committee, was founded in March 1995 by Matt Dorsey, a young political consultant in Washington, D.C. Dorsey's organization, centered around a Web site titled "NewtWatch," was devoted to monitoring the policies of then-House Speaker Newt Gingrich of Georgia. It solicited contributions by credit card, an innovative system at the time.

Dozens of online PACs sprang up in the wake of NewtWatch. Soon, politically active Internet users grew accustomed to giving money online via credit card. By early spring 1999—a full eighteen months before the 2000 election—no fewer than seven presidential candidates were seeking online contributions this way. But it was a risky ploy, because at that time the Federal Election Commission prohibited presidential campaigns from getting matching funds for money donated via credit cards. Matching funds are the lifeblood of presidential campaigns—which are the only campaigns eligible for them—and each candidate in the 2000 presidential race can receive up to $16.75 million. The FEC held, however, that credit card purchases are essentially a loan, and public money shouldn't be used to match loans.

But credit cards are the only way money now changes hands on the Internet, former U.S. Senator and Democrat presidential hopeful Bill Bradley argued in March 1999, when his campaign asked the FEC for an advisory opinion on credit card contributions. Besides, online fundraising can help democratize campaign financing by attracting grassroots contributions, Bradley campaign general counsel Robert F. Bauer wrote in a letter to the Commission.

"The Internet has created an immense opportunity for millions of Americans to participate in the political process," Bauer argued. "Citizens can contribute to a campaign as easily as they can order a book, make an airline reservation, or buy computer software—actions taken thousands of times each day. … At a time of concern over citizen disengagement from the political process, the Commission has the opportunity to ... encourage citizen participation."

Soon after the Bradley campaign made its plea, Vice President Gore, the national Democratic and Republican parties, America Online, and several campaign software makers also came out in support of online contributions. In late May 1999, the FEC released a draft proposal that would allow online credit card contributions to presidential campaigns to be eligible for matching federal funds.

Online fundraising could have a massive impact on the balance of power in political campaigns because it allows candidates who don't have the backing of wealthy supporters and moneyed special interests to compete on the same financial level as those who do. Online contributions come from small donors, true—but those are the toughest and most expensive contributions to garner, political strategists say. Direct mail has traditionally been the only way to raise contributions below $100, and these amounts are partially eaten away by the cost of purchasing mailing lists, printing flyers, and paying for envelopes and postage. In the past, campaigns have had to attract hundreds of thousands of these small contributions in order to make their fundraising efforts profitable.

The cost of maintaining a page on a Web site where donors can make a contribution via credit card can be fairly low, however. Even more important, online contributions appear to attract those voters who may never have been interested in, or capable of, donating money to candidates they favor.

"Internet demographics are younger—and they are new givers. Internet donors are not your typical donor," R. Rebecca Donatelli, chairman of Campaign Solutions, a Virginia-based firm that developed the online contribution system for Sen. McCain's presidential campaign, told *ZDNet News*. Half of the online contributions to the McCain campaign processed by Campaign Solutions in the campaign's early days came from first-time contributors. Of those contributors, 60 percent were less than forty-four years old—much younger than traditional contributors.

Still, like everything else in politics, online fundraising has its own hidden costs. Consultant Donatelli and her partner Tom Hockaday "earned a cut out of every e-dollar McCain raised online," the *Washington Post* reported. Another online fundraising consultant told the *Post* he gets paid for his work by taking a percentage—from 8.5 to 12.5 percent, depending on how much money is raised—off the top of each online contribution as it comes in. Combine that with the cost of maintaining a Web site that must be updated daily, if not hourly, for months on end, and the price tag for chasing donors online can be huge. Publishing millionaire Steve Forbes reportedly spent more than $1 million on high-tech campaigning during his bid for the GOP presidential nomination.

Online fundraising will only get more attractive, however, as Internet technology pervades the homes of more and more voters and drives the overall cost of campaigning down, the experts say. In the 2000 elections, candidates on average paid little more than ten cents for every dollar raised via the Web. In comparison, traditional telemarketing or direct-mail fundraising techniques routinely cost twenty-five to thirty cents (or more!) on the dollar. Online contributions may be unsettling to political strategists steeped in the old habits of pulling in cash via $10,000-a-plate dinners, but they clearly appeal to the upcoming generation of cost-conscious, Internet-savvy candidates and the voters who back them.

Political Polling Online

Political pollsters face an even more immediate threat from the Internet because Net-based political surveys are far cheaper than traditional polls—and they draw more respondents. The Internet has become such an important source of political public opinion, in fact, that Harris Black International, which conducts the widely quoted Harris polls, announced in April 1999 that it would predict the results of primaries and elections in 2000 based on Internet polls.

Informal, click-here-and-tell-us-what-you-think-type polls have become standard on political Web sites in the past several years. Professional pollsters charge that these polls are more or less bogus because they are unscientific—meaning that the responses they draw come from a population of voters that tends to be statistically more homogeneous than the general public. This criticism has some merit. While the demographics of the Internet community have changed dramatically since the early days of Web politicking—when most Internet users were primarily white, affluent, and well educated—there is one statistical characteristic about Internet users that has not changed: They are more politically active than most Americans.

There are other legitimate concerns about Internet-based political polls. First, and most obvious, these polls don't survey Americans who don't own computers. Besides raising the ugly specter of the "digital divide," this criticism points to a second and more insidious problem: the lack of random sampling in Internet polls.

Pollsters using traditional telephone-based polling draw a nationwide sample of voters through a technique called "random-digit dialing," and then weight the responses to mirror the demographics of the population being sampled. According to mathematical theory, the probability is high that the responses obtained in this fashion accurately reflect the attitudes of the entire population.

So far, however, nobody has figured out how to transfer the random sampling technique to the Internet, Mike Traugott, president of the American Association for Public Opinion Research, told the Associated Press during one of the organization's recent annual meetings. Until they do, Internet pollsters will continue to be haunted by a famous survey taken in 1936 that predicted Alf Landon would win the presidential election—and ended up dead wrong when Landon's opponent, Franklin Roosevelt, walked away with the popular vote. Later the press discovered the polling firm had drawn its sample of voters from lists of people who owned telephones and cars—both luxuries in the middle of the Great Depression.

On the other hand, traditional telephone-based polling is facing a growing problem with "nonresponse," or the unwillingness of people to participate in polls. As more and more Americans invest in caller ID and high-tech telephone screening devices, the number of people who have patience for telephone inquiries from strangers—especially during the evening hours when family time is at a premium—is rapidly diminishing, Traugott and other pollsters told the Associated Press. In comparison, Internet polling draws a higher response rate. Couple that with the relatively low cost and rapid response time of Net-based inquiries, and online polling begins to make much more sense, the pollsters say.

Harris Interactive, the online division of Harris Black, for example, accurately predicted the winners in twenty-one of twenty-two elections held in 1998. Few telephone polls matched that accuracy record. Since that time, Net-based polling techniques have improved to the point where adjustments can be made for age, education level, household income, ethnicity, and region of the country, and respondents can be assigned randomly to different parts of the same survey, according to George Terhanian, director of Internet research for Harris Interactive.

Telephone-based Harris polls use about 1,000 respondents, but the Internet-based polls typically use a sample of around 12,000 people, Terhanian told *The Industry Standard*. "Not only do we collect more data quickly but we can ask more questions without burdening any one respondent," he said. Thanks to aggressive efforts to interest Net users in becoming regular poll respondents, Harris Interactive now has a panel of 1.5 million people to query. State-of-the-art sampling and analysis techniques will allow the company to project its findings across the entire population of U.S. voters, according to Terhanian.

No matter how large the sample of voters in an online poll, however, there's no getting around the reality that Net users must essentially volunteer themselves to be part of the survey. Where respondents in traditional polls have always been randomly chosen, an online poll respondent actually has to click on the Harris Interactive Web site and agree to be a virtual guinea pig in order to participate. According to a report in the *Wall Street Journal*, this element of volunteerism makes the partisan skew among Internet users different from the partisan skew among U.S. voters in general. Among Internet users, 34 percent say they are independent voters, 31 percent claim to be Democrats, and 29 percent call themselves Republicans, while the population of "all registered voters" includes 35 percent Democrats, 29 percent Republican, and 28 percent independents.

Online Voter Registration

Ever since the National Voter Registration Act of 1993—often call the "Motor Voter" Act—was passed, the Internet has become a prime source for voter registration. Most states offer online forms that a Net user can download, print out, fill in and sign, and send via regular, or "snail," mail to be registered.

In the elections of the year 2000, however, voter registration actually carried out online began to make headway. The McCain campaign, for example, claimed to have registered over 30,000 voters electronically in California.

The increasing popularity of Internet-aided voter registration is part of a much larger trend toward state and local governments making government services available online, however. Indianapolis residents, for example, can now report abandoned vehicles, dead animals, illegal dumping, and trash pickup problems online, as well as pay their parking tickets. Arizona provides vehicle registration renewals online, while New Mexico not only lets motorists renew their vehicle registrations electronically but also gives residents the option of filing their taxes online. Many cities are also making it possible for contractors to apply for building permits via the Internet. "The motto for the twenty-first century for government should be 'On line, and not in line,'" Jane Hague, a city councilwoman in King County, Washington, told *USA Today*.

A number of cities and counties are also helping their residents get involved in politics by broadcasting government meetings and allowing residents to address public hearings from home. New York City broadcasts Mayor Rudolph Guiliani's press conferences via the Internet, for example, while the Iowa Governor's Strategic Planning Council is collecting feedback via computer from Iowa residents on how the state government should be organized by the year 2010.

The National Governors Association is so enthusiastic about the prospect of online government services that it has established a technology task force chaired by Wyoming Governor Jim Geringer. Giving citizens the ability to communicate by computer "takes government away from being the center of all information," Geringer told *USA Today*. "We put the individual in charge of targeting the information they need."

The more citizens use the Internet to get the government services they need, the more they may become comfortable with online voting and other democratic processes that can be carried out quickly and cheaply via computer. With the passage, in December 2001, of a $2.65 billion bill to modernize the nation's voting systems, who knows? Marc Strassman may turn out to be a prophet.

Chapter 7

Campaign Resources

You want a good metaphor for the Internet, go to Venice in February. You thread your way down foggy streets and over bridges till you lose all sense of compass direction, and then all of a sudden you break into some glorious piazza. The rusty gate on the alley over there might open into a lush garden, and behind that might be a palazzo with long enfilades of rooms and galleries, but you can't see anything from the street. It's a place you get to know as an accumulation of paths and hidden passages, the way a woodsman knows the forest.

—Geoffrey Nunberg, "Virtual Rialto,"
National Public Radio, February 1995

You can't wage a successful grassroots campaign without good information. It's that simple.

If you want to convince Congress, or any other legislative body, to see your side on an issue, you have to come armed with as much data as you can muster to support your argument. You need to be able to explain to lawmakers exactly what you want them to do, why it's in their interest and the interest of their constituents to do it, and how their actions will affect the problems you wish to correct. You ought to be able to answer every question the lawmaker and his or her staff puts to you about your proposal—or know where you can get the answer quickly. Everyone who works with you on the issue, from your co-organizers to the people who read your alerts on the

Net and write or fax Congress or the legislature in response, should be able to do pretty much the same thing.

Why? Because that's the way participatory democracy works. The political scientists will tell you that when government exists at the will of the people, then the people have an obligation to come up with some coherent ideas about what they want government to do.

That's the theory, anyway. The pragmatic answer to why you need quantities of good, solid information to bolster your grassroots campaign is this: Legislatures are chaotic places.

No matter whether you're virtually pacing the halls on Capitol Hill or in a county commission's office suite, you can rest assured that you won't be alone. A lot of other people will be pressing their cases too, so you'll have to work to make your voice heard. And you won't have a lot of time to do it, either. Believe it or not, most elected officials don't have enough staff members to handle all the work that needs doing in the office. You'll most likely have to make your pitch to someone who was supposed to be somewhere else, or was supposed to have completed some other project, a half hour ago.

If, say, you don't know the number and title of the bill you're opposing, or you believe your proposal will benefit schoolchildren but you don't know how many schools there are in the lawmaker's district, then your arguments won't carry much weight. This may not sound fair, but it's the way things work. Again, do you want to have it your way or do you want to be effective?

Luckily, the Net can provide much of the basic information you'll need to bolster your campaign. Some of the best sources of facts, statistics, legislative histories, and reports by experts are only a click of the keyboard away. This chapter looks at some of them.

Political Web Sites

No matter how well organized or technically proficient with computers you are, you won't make a dent in the political process without the correct information. You may have 5,000 people on your legislative alert list ready to call, fax, and e-mail their representatives in the House and the Senate in support of a bill on, say, computer privacy, but if all those messages refer to the wrong bill number, your effort—and theirs—will have been a waste of time. So it's best to get your facts and statistics and addresses straight from the start.

Much of the information you'll need is available on the Web. The following index of Web sites offering material important to an advocacy campaign isn't exhaustive by any means; in fact, this list may not include references that you'll see on plenty of other collections of political sites. That's so for a number of reasons.

I've included only sites that I've seen and used, and that I feel comfortable recommending. In order to make the list, a site has to be reasonably authoritative and easy to understand. It also must be updated regularly. Most important, the organization or government entity that puts up the site has to have an established reputation within the national political community.

You won't find many URLs, however, for the newest brand of political Web site—the for-profit "portal" that offers political information in neat, tailored-just-for-you formats. These eye-catching sites all contain the same sort of information: unedited speeches, statements, and video clips supplied by the candidates and campaigns; position papers written by advocacy organizations; instant polls and e-mail "letters" to local and national officials; automatic mailing lists that will alert voters when their favorite issues come up for debate; and databases of congressional votes and election results against which a site user can compare his or her personal political biases to find a "match" among the slate of hopefuls in any given race.

But beware—these personalized goodies come with a price. Many of these sites are designed primarily to make money, through ad sales, licensing agreements, and fees the campaigns pay to post information. And while most of the political portals promise not to link site users' personally identifying information with slates of issues, the potential for targeting consumers in ways that speak directly to their cherished political beliefs is all too obvious. "Imagine selling ammunition and firearms to voters who oppose gun control," one hot new portal site suggested in a prospectus for potential investors. "Or marketing contraceptives to abortion-rights advocates."

And, finally, a word about government databases. The information the federal government puts up on the Internet has two major advantages: the feds possess some of the most substantive and useful electronic databases any politically active citizen could want, and access to these databases—when access is allowed—is usually free. Always look to federal government sites first when you're organizing information for a campaign. After all, your tax dollars pay for these things.

That's the good news. The bad news is that many government databases are either compilations of raw data, or so poorly organized and nonuser-friendly that they're practically impossible to use unless you're a graduate librarian. Politics has something to do with this state of affairs—remember the hurdles Internet Multicasting Service and the founders of RTKNet had to bridge in order to get government information to a place in cyberspace where everybody could access it? But politics isn't entirely to blame. Bureaucracies move at the speed of glaciers under the best of circumstances, and the federal bureaucracy received its invitation to the Digital Revolution only a few years ago.

Privacy is also a problem with several key federal government sites. For example, the Center for Democracy and Technology (CDT), a respected Washington-based online advocacy group, recently found that just over one-third of federal agencies have privacy policies, and twenty-two federal Web sites have no privacy policy at all. The Veterans Administration (VA), for example, advises visitors that it uses "cookies" —automatic data-collecting programs—to monitor traffic at its sites. Giving notice of cookies is a good practice, but, unfortunately, CDT also found that the VA was downloading actual IP addresses that, in some cases, can be used to identify individual Net users. The Central Intelligence Agency (CIA) didn't have a privacy policy when CDT conducted its survey in mid-April 1999. The CIA *did* include a notice that "Government may monitor and audit the usage of this system, and all persons are hereby notified that use of this system constitutes consent to such monitoring and auditing," but the agency gave no explanation of what it was monitoring, how it was monitoring, or why it was doing so.

The key when visiting a federal government site is to remember that data is being collected that not only can identify you in some fashion but also keeps track, to at least a minimal degree, of which government information you're reading.

If you want to maintain your privacy, don't go to a site, government or otherwise, where it's possible that everybody knows your name. Meanwhile, here are three of the best political Web sites to put on your bookmark list:

THOMAS: Legislative Information on the Internet (http://thomas.loc.gov)

When this innovative database of Congressional information was unveiled at the Library of Congress in January 1995, then-Speaker of the House Newt Gingrich of Georgia promised that it would create "an informed populace that genuinely has access ... to the topic they care about," thus shifting legislative authority away from special interests and into the hands of voters.

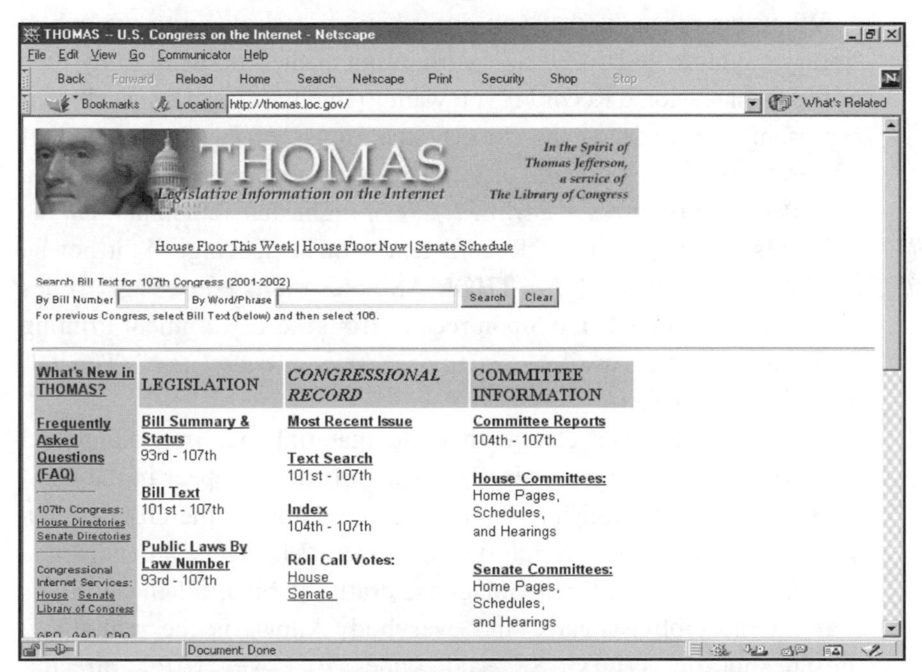

Figure 7.1 THOMAS, the legislative database maintained by the Library of Congress, includes the full *Congressional Record* and Congressional legislation from 1989 to the present.

"Knowledge is power," Gingrich said in a speech at a press conference to unveil THOMAS, which is named for Thomas Jefferson. "Far more than lobbyist reform bills, far more than all the various things that Common Cause says, if every citizen has access to the information that Washington lobbyists have, we will have changed the balance of power in America towards the citizens and out of the Beltway."

That tectonic shift may take a little longer than Gingrich predicted, but THOMAS gives the scales a push. You can search the full text of the Congressional Record here by keyword, and the full text of all the versions of House and Senate bills by either keyword or bill number. If you're looking for pieces of legislation that are generating a lot of controversy, there's "Hot Legislation," a listing searchable by topic, title, or number prepared by analysts from the eminently authoritative Congressional Research Service. Another section of the database presents digests and the legislative histories of bills and their amendments, searchable by keyword, index term, bill or amendment number, sponsor, cosponsor, or committee.

What this means is that you don't have to trek down to the public library anymore and spend hours squinting at the impossibly tiny type of the Congressional Record if you want to find the text of a speech your representative made on the floor of the House or the Senate. And if you're keeping track of a bill as it makes its way through Congress, you can check that progress at any time, day or night. Just remember that the bill texts or Congressional Record texts you're seeking might not be available instantaneously; as THOMAS notes on its home page, "Files are processed immediately upon receipt from the Government Printing Office and are made available when *processing is completed*." (The italics are the author's.)

Some Net activists charge that the material that is available on THOMAS is of little real value because bills don't appear in the database until they're published in an official version by the GPO—often long after the final vote has taken place. "Managers amendments, chairman's marks, recommendations, drafts of bills, all these things that all the lobbyists have and everybody knows is the real thing, they're not on THOMAS," said James P. Love, TAP's director. "Congress has a very cynical attitude. Even though in theory the public is supposed to get access to bills at the same time everybody else gets access, that isn't true at all."

The Vote Smart Web (http://www.vote-smart.org)

Project Vote Smart, a nonprofit organization founded in 1990 at Oregon State University in Corvallis, Oregon, pioneered the art of providing nuts-and-bolts political information on the Net and did it in a fashion that makes its large database one of the most objective, nonpartisan, useful collections of factual information about politicians, the 2000 presidential campaign, political issues, advocacy organizations, and reference materials available anywhere. You can even get research assistance through two 800 numbers.

In years when there are no elections, Project Vote Smart focuses on helping voters monitor the performance of elected officials. "CongressTrack," for example, follows the day-to-day progress of key legislation. Best of all, you don't have to pay a fee for this information or worry about who "owns" it. Project Vote Smart doesn't copyright its publications or database so that "citizens, schools, libraries, and other users may copy and distribute the information freely," according to a

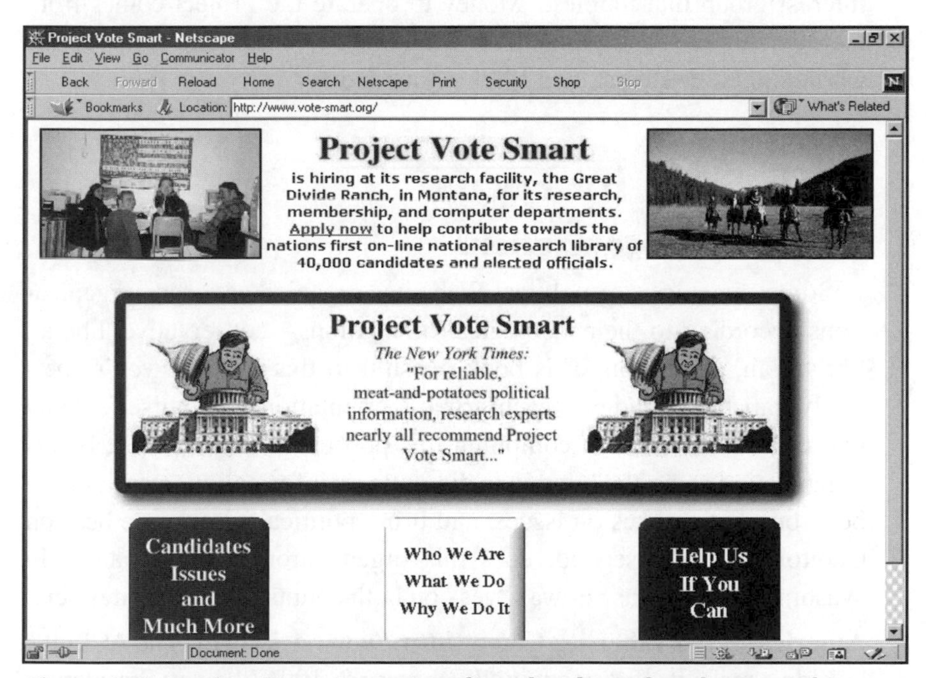

Figure 7.2 Project Vote Smart's online database has been making balanced, solid, and nonpartisan political information available for over a decade.

notice on the Web site. "The Project encourages citizens to share the abundant, accurate information that we assemble and feel is essential to successful self-governance."

Project Vote Smart also takes nonpartisanship very seriously. Former U.S. Senators Edward Brooke, Barry Goldwater, Mark O. Hatfield, Charles Mathias, George McGovern, Frank Moss, and William Proxmire are members of the Project's founding board, as is former Senator and presidential candidate Bill Bradley. The board, the Web site notes, "is balanced between Republicans and Democrats, liberals and conservatives, with some third party members and independents." Of course, as any Washington power player knows, no matter how laudable the careers of board members are, the presence of their names on a letterhead doesn't guarantee that the organization to which they belong won't lean just a little bit this way or that. The proof of Project Vote Smart's nonpartisan intentions lies instead in its refusal to lobby for or against any candidate or issue. Even more important, the Project does not accept funds from government or corporate sources, or "any special interest group that lobbies." Money to operate the Project comes from membership fees and grants from such prestigious organizations as the Carnegie, Ford, Hearst, and Markle foundations.

Web Sites by Focus

Advocacy Organizations

Some directories of political Web sites organize advocacy organizations according to their ideological orientations—conservative, liberal, libertarian, and so on. This book doesn't do that because you're perfectly capable of judging each group's orientation for yourself. Only two criteria mattered in compiling this portion of the list: first, is this organization using the Internet to disseminate information, recruit members, build consensus on issues, and bring political pressure to bear on Capitol Hill; and second, does this organization have a "name" in Washington? The answer was "yes" on both counts for all the sites here.

American Civil Liberties Union (http://www.aclu.org): The ACLU didn't make its Net debut until February 8, 1996, the day President Clinton signed the Telecommunications Reform Act and ushered in a wide-ranging new set of restrictions on electronic speech. No matter.

This is just about as complete a selection of documents, news releases, legal briefs, and Congressional memos on hot civil liberties topics as any activist could want.

Americans for Tax Reform (http://www.atr.org): The free-market, antitax advocacy group headed by well-known libertarian activist Grover Norquist.

The Center for Democracy and Technology (http://www.cdt.org): One of the premier online advocacy organizations on Capitol Hill.

Christian Coalition (http://www.cc.org): The conservative organization founded by former presidential candidate Pat Robertson.

Citizens Against Government Waste (http://www.govt-waste.org): In his first term, President Reagan appointed a blue-ribbon commission, chaired by the late J. Peter Grace, founder of Grace Chemical Co., to "work like tireless bloodhounds to root out government inefficiency and waste of tax dollars." This group carries on the Grace Commission's work, searching out instances of Congressional pork wherever it exists.

The Electronic Frontier Foundation (http://www.eff.org): You might say that EFF kickstarted electronic activism on the national level. Founded in July 1990 by John Perry Barlow, lyricist for the Grateful Dead and a Montana rancher, and Mitchell Kapor, who founded Lotus Development Corp., the producer of the popular spreadsheet software "Lotus 1-2-3," EFF has been at the forefront of cyber-rights issues ever since.

Electronic Privacy Information Center (http://www.epic.org): Founded in 1984, EPIC has become the most aggressively outspoken of the Washington-based advocacy groups lobbying for the privacy rights of Net users and against government control of the Internet.

The Consumer Technology Project (http://www.cptech.org): Founded in the spring of 1995 to address privacy, telecommunications regulation, copyright law, and pharmaceutical drug development and ownership issues, the Consumer Technology Project is one of the two electronic advocacy groups supported by Ralph Nader's CongressWatch organization. The other group follows.

The Congressional Accountability Project (http://www.essential.org/orgs/CAP/CAP.html), which has pressed for a greater range of congressional information online.

City and County

The Institute of Government, at the University of North Carolina at Chapel Hill (http://ncinfo.iog.unc.edu): A great resource for state and local government information on the Web, this site also includes an exhaustive listing of North Carolina government Web sites as well as a cleverly designed set of links to federal government information.

National Association of Counties (http://www.naco.org): Formed in the midst of the Great Depression, this organization now represents almost two-thirds of the more than 3,000 county governments across the country.

National League of Cities (http://www.nlc.org): This organization has been representing the interests of municipal governments since its founding in 1924. It's dedicated to "advancing the public interest, building democracy and community, and improving the quality of life by strengthening the performance and capabilities of local governments and advocating the interests of local communities."

Congress

House of Representatives Home Page (http://www.house.gov): Founded in early 1994, this site has grown from a skimpy collection of links on remote House servers to a full-fledged resource worthy of taxpayer dollars (or, at least, *some* of them). There are calendars for the House's daily and weekly floor schedule, the annual Congressional schedule and committee hearing schedules; links to member, committee, and leadership offices, as well as to House commissions and task forces; and an interactive database of roll call votes, as composed under the direction of the Clerk of the House, since 1990. But be forewarned: You can't get the e-mail addresses for a number of House Members here. The lack of e-mail links is startling when those addresses are available on hundreds of commercial political Web sites.

The United States Senate's World Wide Web Server (http://www.senate.gov): The Senate may be "the world's greatest deliberative body," as the old Washington phrase terms it, but that doesn't mean that the Senate has always been technologically hip. The Senate's Sergeant at Arms established a gopher in the spring of 1994, but the Senate didn't upgrade its technology—or the information that technology offered—for another eighteen months. The House of Representatives inaugurated THOMAS in January 1995, but only in October—almost ten months later—did the Senate introduce its own Web site after Senate Rules Committee chairman John R. Warner of Virginia insisted on it. The Senate reportedly feared that its members would become victims of "spoofing," a hacker trick where someone is able to intercept an electronic message on its way through the Internet, change the message's wording, and send it back on its way. Supposedly a well-executed spoof is impossible to trace.

Documents

GPO Access on the Web (http://thorplus.lib.purdue.edu/gpo): This site has won raves from just about everybody who's reviewed it. Purdue University, which developed this site, thoughtfully provides links to more than a dozen GPO databases, including the Congressional Record, the Federal Register, and reports from the General Accounting Office, Congress' in-house number crunchers.

Gutenberg (http://www.gutenberg.net/): Just about every historical American document is here in electronic form. The list includes the Federalist Papers, the Constitution, the Declaration of Independence, the Gettysburg Address, and several Presidential Inaugural Addresses, but it doesn't stop there.

The National Archives Information Server (http://www.nara.gov): Don't judge this book by its cover—or by its monumentally clumsy lists, for that matter. The National Archives has kept federal records for more than 200 years, meaning it's another one of those just plain invaluable places to put on your bookmark list.

Federal Government

NOTE that those sites with a "clearly labeled" privacy policy, according to the Center for Democracy and Technology survey, are marked with an asterisk (*).

Cabinet Departments

Department of Agriculture (http://www.usda.gov)

***Department of Commerce (http://www.doc.gov)**

***Department of Defense (http://www.defenselink.mil)**: Here's where you'll find the "Early Bird," the Pentagon's daily compilation of leading news stories about the military. (Washington reporters who follow the Pentagon's activities keep up with the Early Bird. It's not the news that's important but the selection of stories—which articles the editors include and which ones they leave out—that sometimes offers a clue to the latest policy concern among the Defense Department's top brass.)

Department of Education (http://www.ed.gov)

Department of Energy (http://home.doe.gov)

Department of Health and Human Services (http://www.os.dhhs.gov)

***Department of Housing and Urban Development (http://www.hud.gov)**

***Department of Interior (http://www.doi.gov)**

***Department of Justice (http://www.usdoj.gov)**

Department of Labor (http://www.dol.gov)

Department of State (http://www.state.gov)

Department of Transportation (http://www.dot.gov)

Department of Treasury (http://www.ustreas.gov)

Veterans Affairs (http://www.va.gov)

Other Major Independent and Regulatory Agencies

Central Intelligence Agency (http://www.odci.gov)

Commodity Futures Trading Commission (http://www.cftc.gov)

Consumer Product Safety Commission (http://www.cpsc.gov)

Environmental Protection Agency (http://www.epa.gov)

Federal Communications Commission (http://www.fcc.gov)

***Federal Deposit Insurance Company (http://www.fdic.gov)**

Federal Election Commission (http://www.fec.gov)

***Federal Trade Commission (http://www.ftc.gov)**

***General Services Administration (http://www.gsa.gov)**

***National Aeronautics and Space Administration (http://www.nasa.gov)**

***National Archives and Records Administration (http://www.nara.gov)**

National Endowment for the Arts (http://arts.endow.gov)

National Endowment for the Humanities (http://ns1.neh.fed.us)

National Institutes of Health (http://www.nih.gov)

National Security Agency (http://www.nsa.gov)

National Science Foundation (http://www.nsf.gov)

National Telecommunications and Information Administration (http://www.ntia.doc.gov)

Nuclear Regulatory Commission (http://www.nrc.gov)

***Security and Exchange Commission (http://www.sec.gov)**

Small Business Administration (http://www.sba.gov)

Smithsonian Institution (http://www.si.edu)

Social Security Administration (http://www.ssa.gov)

United States Agency for International Development (http://www.usia.gov)

***United States Information Agency (http://www.usia.gov)**

United States Postal Service (http://www.usps.gov)

Voice of America (http://www.voa.gov)

Other Key Federal Government Sites and Databases

Internal Revenue Service (http://www.irs.ustreas.gov/prod)

Federal Bureau of Investigation (http://www.fbi.gov)

Federal Emergency Management Agency (http://www.fema.gov)

Fedworld Information Network (http://www.fedworld.gov): Begun as an experiment in November 1992 on small dial-up access system that cost only about $40,000, this site is now a good source if you're trying to track down obscure—and some not-so-obscure—federal government documents. Tucked in between databases of U.S. Customs rulings and the catalogue of the National Audiovisual Center, for example, you'll find the EPA's Clean Air Act database and the decisions of the U.S. Supreme Court from 1937–1975. (Don't scoff at the court decisions—have you paid to do legal research on a commercial database lately?)

General Accounting Office (http://www.gao.gov)

U.S. Census Bureau (http://www.census.gov)

The White House (http://www.whitehouse.gov)

General Political Information

AllPolitics (http://AllPolitics.com): A general political database put together by CNN and *Time* magazine, including a broad range of political coverage as well as a "Virtual Primary" for presidential candidates.

America Online "Government Guide" (http://www.government guide.com): This area of AOL provides the now-standard congressional information search engine, based on ZIP Codes, as well as an e-mail-to-Congress service and a mechanism through which Net users can track their Congressional representatives' votes. Also included: a very useful guide to federal, state, and local resources in your area, organized by an interactive, Zip Code-driven database.

DebateUSA (http://www.debateusa.com): The strength of this somewhat chaotic site lies in its long list of political-news headlines, complete with dates and publications, and its page on statewide ballot measures.

ELECnet (http://www.debexar.com/elecnet): This Web site has hundreds of links to state, county, and city election-related sites in all fifty states as well as a listing of federal, state, and local election offices on the Internet. It also connects to a listing of federal agencies that provide election-related information.

evote.com (http://www.evote.com): This interesting but understated site will surprise you. In a few spare strokes, evote.com manages to hit all the topics that really matter in the current game of politics: news, players, polls, "election 2000," and "who's in/out." Worth a look.

FECInfo (http://www.tray.com/fecinfo): Tony Raymond, the Federal Election Commission's first Webmaster, launched this site in 1996 when the FEC bureaucracy moved too slowly to take advantage of what Raymond considered the best of the Internet's numbers-crunching capabilities. Now you'll find here a host of slice-'n-dice data combinations, all based on the FEC's official database—campaign contributors' names, ZIP Codes, and occupations; PACs and Party Committees; lobbying registrations; U.S. House and Senate campaign expenditures—plus an advanced database on "soft money" contributions (the donations for which federal law doesn't require a report) from 1997 on.

The Freedom Forum (http://www.freedomforum.org): Once called the Gannett Foundation for its connection to the Gannett newspaper chain, the Freedom Forum underwrites a variety of activities aimed at improving American journalism, including seminars, fellowships for mid-career and foreign journalists, and the Freedom Forum Media Studies Center at Columbia University in New York.

League of Women Voters Education Fund (http://www.lwv.org): Founded in 1920 to advance women's right to vote, the League of Women Voters is a multi-issue organization whose mission is to encourage the informed and active participation of citizens in government and to influence public policy through education and advocacy. Information pertaining to local state chapters can be found on the Web site.

National Political Index (http://www.politicalindex.com): A truly remarkable index to just about every bit of political information that exists on the Web. A must for basic research.

Political Information.com (http://www.politicalinformation.com): A political and policy search engine, this site sports links more than 4,000 online resources for political topics. Updated frequently, it also contains congressional schedules.

Politics.Com (http://www.politics.com): Never bookmark a political Web site again if you've got this site! If you can't find that great collection of political cartoons or the database on left-handed urban twenty-something independents, Politics.com's likely to have a link to it, as well as links to just about every other topic a politics-obsessed heart can desire.

Politics1 (http://www.politics1.com): Any political Web site that's been endorsed by both PBS and Fox News must have across-the-political-spectrum appeal. This site contains the standard items—links to and information on the 2000 presidential campaigns, congressional and state races, political parties, "hot" issues and political news—but its approach is winningly balanced and non-partisan.

Politics Online (http://www.politicsonline.com): This site, founded by politics-on-the-Net pioneer and campaign consultant Phil Noble, is the home to the Weekly Politicker and NetPulse, the excellent mailing lists noted later in this chapter. Most of the materials here are the same, but you can download the full reports instead of reading one-paragraph blurbs as you do in the newsletters. Don't miss the foreign campaign commentary from Noble, who has done extensive political consulting in both Europe and South America.

Rock the Vote (http://www.rockthevote.org): This four-year-old MTV-founded political Web site, which once seemed more hip than politically savvy, has grown up. Still eye-catching, Rock the Vote has branched out from voter registration, its original mission, to political and community activism.

Voter Information Services (http://www.vis.org): Founded in 1995, VIS continues to offer a straightforward collection of databases on Congressional voting records, both with and without advocacy organization voting "score cards." If you want to know who voted for or against a key bill, search here first.

Media

Television and Radio

ABC News.com "Political Nation" (http://www.abcnews.go.com/sections/politics): Part of the regular ABC News site, Political Nation is an excellent spot to research the very latest feint and thrust on the national political scene.

CBS.Com—News (http://cbsnews.cbs.com): This comprehensive news site offers editorial coverage on the latest issues organized by such categories as national, world, health, "scitech," and "Eye on Politics."

C-SPAN (http://www.c-span.org): C-SPAN, the lifeblood of any true-blue political junkie, is also available on the Web.

MSNBC News (http://www.msnbc.com/news/POLITICS_front.asp): An unusually interactive site, the MSNBC Politics page provides a "get involved" section with a guide to Congress, an e-mail-your-representative feature, and a political bulletin board where voters can share thoughts about current issues. Its continuously updated news section includes, at this writing, a "Decision 2000" page composed of an interesting and informative combination of news, analysis, and public opinion research.

National Public Radio (http://www.npr.org): For die-hard NPR fans, news headlines in RealAudio, or audio-on-demand, format.

PBS Online (http://www.pbs.org): If you missed your daily fix of the "The NewsHour with Jim Lehrer," don't fret. It's all here in hypertext and terrific graphics.

Newspapers

AJR NewsLink (http://ajr.newslink.org): Another entrant in the "most comprehensive" category, this site purports to contain 9,000 links to "newspapers, magazines, broadcasters, and news services worldwide." Run by the well-regarded American Journalism Review, this is a news junkie's heaven.

Associated Press (http://wire.ap.org): The WIRE is the news Web site of the Associated Press, its member newspapers, and broadcasters. To enter the site, visitors choose from AP member newspapers, from across the country that are listed by geographical regions and states.

Newspaperlinks.com (http://newspaperlinks.com): Compiled by the Newspaper Association of America, this site is an index of the more than 850 local newspapers found on the Web. No matter where Internet users live, they may find that their trusted source for news and information is available online with comprehensive coverage for local political races and election results.

Roll Call Online (http://www.rollcall.com): This is the online version of the twice-weekly Capitol Hill newspaper that is "must" reading for anyone who works for or lobbies Congress. It also includes a "Hill Directory" that is one of the best around.

The Hill (http://www.hillnews.com): Founded in 1994 by former *New York Times* reporter Martin Tolchin, *The Hill* is the Johnny-come-lately to coverage of Capitol Hill. But don't overlook it—its scrappy reporting style is always fun to read, and it often goes scoop-for-scoop with its more-established competitor, *Roll Call*.

Online Press

Salon (http://www.salon.com): Irreverent, sharp, entertaining, hip—plus some of the best writing anywhere (not just on the Web). The political coverage is always intriguing.

Wired (http://www.wired.com): This is the e-zine version of *Wired* magazine, which has become the popular bible of the Information Age—and a good, if libertarian-minded, source of news of political issues impacting the Net.

Magazines

Business Week Online (http://www.businessweek.com): Business Week concentrates on the corporate side of the news. But its reports on the high-tech industry are worth even a political activist's time because of what they reveal about Silicon Valley's view of the political process.

Campaign and Elections (http://www.campaignline.com): It may be dry and somewhat technical, and its businesslike approach to campaigning may unsettle neophytes for whom politics is still a labor of love, but this magazine is on everybody's desk in Washington.

The Economist (http://www.economist.com): Some of the freshest and most biting commentary on American politics to be found outside U.S. borders. Besides, reading *The Economist* regularly is considered a sign of extreme connectedness among conservative Beltway insiders.

IntellectualCapital.com (http://intellectualcapital.com/politics): IntellectualCapital.com is a relatively new weekly e-zine focusing on public policy and opinion, with a Washington twist.

Mother Jones (http://www.motherjones.com): Again, if you want left wing, political, and hip, this is it.

Newsweek (http://www.newsweek.com): One of the "big three" newsmagazines. If you really want to be active in politics—online or off—you have to monitor at least one of these news outlets.

Time.Com (http://www.time.com/time): Not only is *Time* the leader of the "big three" newsmagazines, but it was one of the first of the so-called traditional media to forge a place on the Web.

U.S. News & World Report Online (http://www.USnews.com/usnews): The third member of the "big three," with a growing online presence.

Political Parties

Democrats

Democratic National Committee (DNC) (http://www.democrats.org): Campaigns tend to dominate this site (as they dominate the Republican National Committee site) but you'll also find plenty of information on current legislation, policy issues in the news, and local party organizations and their activities. If you want free Internet access, and you don't find it disconcerting to have a national political party as your ISP, click on the links to FreeDem.com.

The House Democratic Caucus (http://dcaucusweb.house.gov): Includes current news, charts comparing various "flat tax" plans proposed by leaders on both sides of the aisle and links to Democratic House Members—all aimed at promoting the Democratic agenda.

House Democratic Leadership (http://democraticleader.house.gov): Offers updates on current legislation, profiles of Democratic leaders, and press releases.

Senate Democratic Policy Committee (http://www.senate.gov/~dpc): This committee promotes the Democratic agenda in the Senate, just as the Democratic Caucus does in the House.

Republicans

Freedom Works: Office of the House Majority Leader (http://freedom.house.gov): Offers news releases on and analyses of policy initiatives, updates on current legislation, a schedule for the weekly radio address by GOP House members, and a House calendar.

House Republican Conference (http://www.gop.gov): Includes hot topics as they occur in the course of the day-to-day work of promoting the Republican agenda in the House.

The Senate Republican Policy Committee (http://www.senate.gov/~rpc): Promotes the Republican agenda in the Senate just as the House Republican Conference does on its side of Capitol Hill.

The Senate Republican Conference (http://www.senate.gov/~src): Provides links to the Web sites maintained by Republican Senators, as well as to such Congressional databases as THOMAS and the Senate Republican Policy Committee's archive of its newsletters.

The Republican National Committee (http://www.rnc.org): Again, campaigns rule here (Isn't that what national political parties are all about?), but if you want information on all things GOP, it's here. And if you're a multimedia fan, click on GOPTV, a grab bag of video news briefs, political television ads, special reports, and "week in review" clips.

Third Parties

Green Party (http://www.greens.org)

Libertarian Party (http://www.lp.org)

Reform Party (http://www.reform-party-usa.org): The wing of the Reform Party that nominated Patrick J. Buchanan for president in 2000.

Socialist.Org (http://www.biblio.org/spc/index.html)

United We Stand America (http://www.uwsa.com)

States

The Council of State Governments (http://www.statesnews.org): Based in the beautiful bluegrass country of Lexington, Kentucky, this organization is the foremost location for state government information in the country.

National Conference of State Legislatures (http://www.ncsl.org): Includes listings of state legislatures, NCSL services and news, and analyses of state-federal relations. One of the most active national organizations on the Washington scene in the arena of state concerns.

Think Tanks

The Aspen Institute (http://www.aspeninst.org): If you're looking for heavyweight policy debates that sometimes verge on the esoteric, this is the place.

The Benton Foundation (http://www.benton.org): The Washington-based Benton Foundation promotes "public interest values and noncommercial services" on the Net.

The Brookings Institution (http://www.brook.edu): The venerable Brookings, Washington's premier policy wonk domain, comes to the Net.

Cato Institute (http://www.cato.org): The libertarian voice on the Washington policy scene.

The Heritage Foundation (http://www.townhall.com): A well-established and well-regarded incubator for conservative thought, the Heritage Foundation has become the equivalent of an ideas machine for the Republicans in the House and Senate.

The Progress and Freedom Foundation (http://www.pff.org): Founded in 1993 by Jeffrey A. Eisenach, once an aide to former House Speaker Newt Gingrich of Georgia, the Washington-based PFF has quickly become a bigfoot in Washington policy circles that focus on Net-based issues.

New Democrats Online (http://www.ndol.org): Created by the Democratic Leadership Council, the middle-of-the-road group that coined the term "New Democrat," this site is the online home of the Progressive Policy Institute, the Democrats' outlet for "progressive ideas, mainstream values, and nonbureaucratic approaches to governing."

State-Based Think Tanks (http://www.cascadepolicy.org/spn.htm): As this site notes, this is a "fairly complete" state-by-state list of "free-market-oriented," state-based think tanks.

RAND Corporation (http://www.rand.org): This California think tank has been riding the cutting edge of strategic thought on technological and defense issues for more than four decades. Rand was predicting the growth of a worldwide computer network when Steve Jobs was still working out of his garage.

Electronic Mailing Lists

Ironically, for all the phenomenal growth of the World Wide Web and the growing popularity of both nonprofit and for-profit political Web sites, the electronic mailing list remains one of the best sources of up-to-the-minute information on political issues. And the good news is that all you need to tap into the power of these lists is an e-mail address.

Electronic lists operate exactly the same way regular mailing lists do. They contain the names and addresses of people who want to keep up with the day-to-day debate on a particular issue; their "owners," or operators, send the people on the list legislative information, from voting records and reports to transcripts of floor dialogue, as soon as it's available. When that data goes out through the post office—as it does on a regular mailing list—it may not arrive in list members' hands for twenty-four hours or more. With e-mail, the data arrives within seconds.

Subscribing to an electronic mailing list is also the easiest way to make sure you'll know about important political issues at almost the same time they surface in Congress or your state legislature. Many list owners also lobby for or conduct research on the issues around which the list has been designed, which means they're often privy to the latest legislative scoop and anxious to get that information out to other people who have the same interest.

Here are a few general guidelines for subscribing to a mailing list.. You'll receive similar instructions every time you sign on to a list, so what may seem like gobbledygook at first glance will soon become stultifyingly familiar.

To subscribe, send e-mail to one of the following:

[list name]-request@[list address]
listserv@[list address]
majordomo@[list address]
listserver@[address]
owner-[list name]@[list address]

Do not—repeat, do not—send a subscription request to the list name by itself. What you'll be doing in effect is messaging everybody on the list that you want to subscribe, and you're almost guaranteed to get some nasty messages back from other subscribers.

Your e-mail message should be simply SUBSCRIBE [list name] [your first name][your last name], but if that doesn't work, try SUBSCRIBE [listname].

If you aren't getting anywhere with your subscription request send "HELP" to the request address; write "HELP" on the subject line of your message, not in the body of it. When all else fails, send a message to postmaster@[list address] asking for help.

And if you're not satisfied with the listings here, try these Web-based directories:

- **Directory of Political Discussion Listservers (http://www.nova.edu/Inter-Links/cgi-bin/lists)**
- **Search The List of Lists (http://catalog.com/vivian/interest-group-search.html)**
- **Liszt (http://www.liszt.com)**
- **eGroups (http://www.egroups.com)**
- **Topica (http://www.topica.com)**

The Association for Interactive Media (AIM) bills itself as "the inside-the-Beltway lobbying representation for the Internet industry." Its claim that "no other Internet organization is more connected in the Washington power structure" should be judged in light of the activities of other lobbying groups you'll find in the following pages. Still, AIM offers several interesting and informative online newsletters, including:

AIM's Research Update Service, a compendium of summaries of research on the Internet marketplace. To subscribe, send a blank message to: join-research@lists.interactivehq.org.

AIM's Who's News, which the group touts as "your guide to deals, dealmakers, movers, and shakers." To subscribe, send a blank message to: join-whosnews@lists.interactivehq.org.

AIM's Internet Politics Insider, a daily update of Internet events and technology policy happenings on Capitol Hill. To subscribe, send a blank message to: subscribe-politics@lists.interactivehq.org.

CDT Policy Posts, a publication of the Center for Democracy and Technology, aims "to keep you informed on developments in public policy issues affecting civil liberties online." To subscribe, send a message to: majordomo@cdt.org with "subscribe policy-posts" in the body of the message.

Democracies Online Newswire, run by Steven Clift, a longtime member of Minnesota E-Democracy, tracks grassroots political projects all over the world. To subscribe, send a message to: listserv@tc.umn.edu with "SUB DO-WIRE" in the body of the message. Clift's archives, an excellent resource for grassroots organizers who want to see what other communities have done, are also available on the Web (**http://www.e-democracy.org/do**).

Digital Democracy, Marc Strassman's electronic discussion list that tracks online voting projects. Join this e-mail list at **http://digitaldemocracy.listbot.com**.

The EPIC Alert is a free biweekly publication of the Electronic Privacy Information Center, a public interest research center in Washington established in 1994 to "focus public attention on emerging privacy issues." To subscribe, send a message to: epicnews@epic.org with the subject: "subscribe."

GovAccess, published since 1990 by electronic activist Jim Warren, has got to be one of the most innovative and opinionated political mailing lists to be found anywhere on the Net. Warren says his list distributes "irregular info & advocacy regarding technology and civil liberties, citizen access to government—and government access to citizens, covert and overt." There's a little discussion here, in the form of reader feedback, but it's mainly Warren's show. To subscribe, send a message to Majordomo@well.com. Archives for GovAccess are available on the Web at **http://www.cpsr.org/cpsr/states/california/govaccess**.

Politech, the mailing list maintained by Wired Washington bureau chief Declan McCullagh, has been chronicling the peculiar mix of politics and technology in the nation's Capital since the early days. Politech is "strictly moderated," Declan notes in the subscription information—and he means it. To subscribe, send a message to: majordomo@vorlon.mit.edu.

Red Rock Eater News Service, maintained by Internet wunderkind Phil Agre, a professor in the University of California at San Diego's communications department, is a sort of running dialogue on Net culture, rather than an issue-oriented mailing list. Discussion here is one-way, from Agre to his subscribers, but the messages are always insightful and well written. *The Network Observer*, Agre's essays on the nature of government in the Information Age, is also distributed through RRE. To subscribe to RRE, send a message to: rre-request@weber.ucsd.edu, with "subscribe [your first name][your last name]" in the subject line. [The name "Red Rock Eater," by the way, comes from thc following passage in Bennett Cerf's Book of Riddles:
Q: What is big and red and eats rocks?
A: A big red rock eater.
"When I was four years old I thought this was hilarious," Agre notes.]

The Weekly Politicker, a weekly online newsletter published by PoliticsOnline, which was in turn founded by politics-on-the-Internet pioneer and political consultant Phil Noble. Full of nifty news briefs on the latest in online voting, online campaigns, political Web sites, Web-based political fundraising—you name it. To subscribe, send a blank message to: politicker-request@politicsonline.com. If you like the Politicker, try subscribing also to

NetPulse, a biweekly online journal that will tell you (almost) more than you ever wanted to know about the growing realm of political activity on the Internet. To subscribe, send a blank message to: netpulse-request@politicsonline.com. At this writing, subscriptions to NetPulse were still free, but PoliticsOnline may begin charging a subscription fee in the future.

The Democratic National Committee mailing lists

Democratic News, which includes regular DNC briefings, press releases, party publications, and information about candidates, events, and issues. To subscribe, send a message to: majordomo@democrats.org with "subscribe news" in the body of the message.

Democratic News Digest, published weekly, which compiles the contents of Democratic News each week and sends them in a single e-mail message. To subscribe, send a message to: majordomo@democrats.org with "subscribe news digest" in the body of the message.

Democratic Events, which includes a monthly calendar of events from the DNC's Secretary, as well as alerts to special events like televised Presidential addresses. To subscribe, send a message to: majordomo@democrats.org with "subscribe event" in the body of the message.

The Republican National Committee mailing lists

The RNC Monday Briefing, an eight-page newsletter with a calendar of upcoming events, poll results, and excerpts from newspaper editorials and columnists. Send a message to: majordomo@rnc.org with "subscribe briefinglist" in the body of the message.

Press Releases, which distributes press releases and issue briefings, include a section that contrasts quotes from President Clinton's speeches with his record. Send a message to: majordomo@rnc.org with "subscribe presslist" in the body of the message.

"Rising Tide," which includes information about the television program of the same name that is produced by GOP-TV. Send a message to: majordomo@rnc.org with "subscribe goptvlist" in the body of the message.

Chapter 8

The Virtual Campaign Trail

The Internet is not about technology. It's about relationships.

—Phil Madsen, Ventura campaign Webmaster, in "Notes Regarding Jesse Ventura's Internet Use in his 1998 Campaign for Minnesota Governor."

Former Senator Robert Dole of Kansas, the Republican nominee for president, looked directly into the television camera at the end of the first presidential debate of 1996 and delivered a historic message. "I ask for your support, I ask for your help," Dole said to the millions of Americans watching him, "and if you really want to get involved, just tap into my home page: www.dolekemp96org."

From the moment the first campaign bunting went up on the first roughshod podium in New Hampshire in 1996, online journalists began calling that year's presidential campaign "the last election of the Industrial Age." Dole—who bumbled his own URL by leaving out the last "dot"—may himself have been ambivalent about crossing into the Information Age, but a number of other politicians were not.

The 1996 Campaign Online

Personal computers made their debut in the late 1970s, and by the 1992 election, millions of Americans had PCs in their homes. But the Internet wasn't even a factor in that year's campaign equation. The World Wide Web was in its infancy in 1992; only a few thousand computer researchers and academics even understood how it operated. More important, few Americans had modems fast enough to make it practical to access political information on the Net. Modem speeds of 2,400-baud were still the standard for most home PCs; only diehard computer enthusiasts were investing in the new 14,400-baud modems back then.

How different things were by 1996! The Web was growing at mind-boggling rates each month, and 28,800-baud modems had become the standard for home PCs. More than ten million Americans went online through commercial online services such as CompuServe and America Online, and several million more communicated via e-mail and surfed the Web regularly through direct Internet connections either at work or at home. By the time Dole and President Bill Clinton went head-to-head on national TV in early October, both campaigns were actively soliciting votes through Web sites, while hundreds of other candidates nationwide were doing the same. Despite Dole's gaffe, so many Net users tried to access his campaign site after the first debate that the site was jammed for several hours.

Grassroots Organizing in 1996

For the most part, grassroots organizations rested on their technical laurels and simply expanded their use of the Internet during the 1996 election year. Petitions became a standard on many politically oriented Web sites, as did pointers on effective political action for the uninitiated. "At a minimum, get your friends and family registered, out to vote, and members of the NRA (National Rifle Association). That's what won us the November 1994 election," Jeff Chan, the originator of CA-FIREARMS, the electronic mailing list that played a major role in the recall campaign against California State Senator Roberti, advised readers of his new Web site, RKBA.org: Arms Rights and Liberty Information on the Internet.

In fact, the most telling political element on the Net during 1996 was the emergence of measurable support online for third-party candidates. Harry Browne, the Libertarian Party's presidential nominee, for example, was all but ignored in the mainstream media despite his $3 million campaign war chest and the fact that his name was on the ballot in all fifty states. On the Net, however, Browne at least had the veneer of a winner. According to the Browne campaign, the Libertarian candidate "cyberwhipped" Bill Clinton and Bob Dole in eleven of eighteen Internet-based presidential polls.

Irrepressible third-party candidate Ross Perot had talked about "electronic town halls" and Internet-based political communications during the 1992 election, long before any other national candidate did. Four years later, Perot's newly minted Reform Party took the innovative step of allowing its members to vote online to nominate the party's presidential candidate. Anyone who signed a petition to place the party on a state ballot received a personal identification number allowing them access to an electronic ballot through the party's Web site. Using a personal identification number, or "PIN," Party members could vote for either Perot or Colorado Governor Richard Lamm. Another Perot-affiliated political group, United We Stand America, used the Internet to great effect in 1996 to recruit and coordinate with members.

Neither the Browne nor the Perot/Reform Party efforts really mark the end of "old-media" politics and the rise of Information Age politics, however. The Browne campaign was certainly prescient in its use of e-mail to communicate with voters and raise campaign funds. On the other hand, Browne benefited mightily from the skewed demographics of the Web in 1996. In a survey where Browne beat Clinton 45-33 percent, for example, more than one-third of the voters identified themselves as Libertarians. Most political pollsters will tell you that registered Republicans and Democrats—and independent voters—always far outnumber Libertarians in exit polls on Election Day. As for the Reform Party's online voting system, it proved disappointing in the final analysis: less than five percent of the more than 49,000 votes cast for the Party's nomination were cast online.

Listening to Congress

That isn't to imply that the 1996 election brought political groundbreaking on the Internet to a halt, however. Congress isn't exactly a "grassroots organization," but thanks to Sen. Conrad Burns, R-Mont., the most important innovation in political consensus building via the Net to make its appearance that year happened right on Capitol Hill. Burns, the sponsor of a bill to ease federal restrictions on the export of encryption software, helped several online advocacy groups make history by lending his support to the first full-blown "cybercasts" of congressional committee hearings in June and July 1996.

When the Senate Commerce, Science, and Transportation Committee's subcommittee on science, technology, and space took up Burns's encryption bill on June 26, 1996, the entire proceedings were broadcast live over the Internet. Chat rooms, where Net users could pose questions for members of the committee to ask witnesses, were also set up. When the full Senate Commerce Committee considered the bill a month later, Matt Raymond, a member of Burns's staff, and Jonah Seiger, a policy analyst for the Washington-based Center for Democracy and Technology, monitored the chat rooms and wrote down the questions for interns to pass along to committee members as the hearings progressed.

As they "chatted" or listened, Net users could also browse through extensive background material on both the encryption issue and the witnesses at the hearings provided by Hotwired, *Wired* magazine's Web site, which cosponsored the broadcasts. More than 1,000 people listened to the broadcast of the second hearing, and Seiger estimated that there were at least forty Net users in the chat room at any one time. "The possibilities for interaction between Americans and their elected representatives are just endless in a format like this," he said.

The Net community's response to the cybercasts differed dramatically from its response to many of the politically oriented Web sites that sprang up during the 1996 campaign. Many of those sites offered only one-way communication—from the candidate to interested voters—and failed to draw government closer to the public the way some optimistic online advocates predicted would happen as the election cycle got underway.

A number of scholars saw the failure of interactivity in the 1996 campaign sites as irrefutable evidence that the Net wouldn't become a tool of participatory democracy anytime soon. "The idea was that parties and interest groups would become less important because people would be able to communicate directly with government, and government would know what people want," Bruce Bimber, a professor of political science at the University of California at Santa Barbara, was quoted as saying in an Associated Press report. "That's almost a Utopian view."

Candidates in the 1996 elections didn't have the time to answer "any kind of mail, let alone e-mail," added Richard Brody, professor emeritus of political science at Stanford University. "They'll usually wrench themselves away from whatever they're doing to see someone who's going to give them money," he told the AP. "But anyone writing even a very reasoned [electronic] letter and expecting to get an interchange from anyone even close to the candidate strikes me as being foolish."

Even as scholars were pooh-poohing the Net's potential for political interaction, one of the largest and most Net-savvy political groups in the nation was putting computer technology to extremely effective use in that stew-pot of political intrigue, the quadrennial party convention. In August 1996, when rumors spread on the floor of the Republican Convention that delegates who were members of the Christian Coalition would walk out during the keynote speech by Representative Susan Molinari of New York, an abortion-rights supporter, coalition strategists signaled their members via handheld computers to stay put. From a hotel room off the convention site, the powers-that-be of the 1.7-million-member coalition wrote messages with a stylus on Personal Digital Assistants and flashed the messages to thirteen floor managers, or "whips," who each then passed the messages on to six to eight assistant managers, who in turn would spread the word among up to twenty delegates each. The PDAs became the fastest method of communication among the far-flung managers and coalition strategists because convention rules banned cell phones from the hall. "If there had been a floor demonstration or a minority platform introduced, we needed the technology … to mobilize our people literally in a few minutes," coalition spokesman Mike Russell said.

Candidates on the Web

Did having an Internet presence assure candidates that they would be victorious at the polls? It's hard to make a definitive answer one way or the other. A significant percentage of the winners in the 1996 Congressional faces were Net savvy: More than a third of the seventy-four Republicans and Democrats who were elected to the House for the first time that year put up campaign Web sites, as did seven of the fifteen candidates who won seats in the Senate.

Some aides to these winners believed the Web provided their bosses a margin of victory. Democrat Walter H. Capps, for example, ran against Rep. Andrea Seastrand, R-Calif., for the first time in 1994 and lost to her by 1,600 votes. Kenneth A. Owens, a Capps campaign volunteer who designed a Web site for Capps's 1996 rematch against Seastrand, said the site made a huge difference the second time around. Capps beat Seastrand in 1996 by some 12,000 votes. "Since we had around 20,000 visits to our Web site, I think it can definitely be said that the Internet helped contribute to that winning margin," Owens said.

In Virginia, high-tech entrepreneur Mark Warner went, in a period of ten months, from being a political unknown who was regarded in some corners as the Democratic Party's "desperation" challenger to incumbent Republican Senator John W. Warner, to a real threat to John Warner's primacy in the Senate (Republican Warner beat Democrat Warner by only six percent of the vote). The thousands of dollars in his own money that Mark Warner spent on the campaign certainly did a lot to boost his standing, but his Internet efforts can't be overlooked either.

The "Mark Warner for U.S. Senate" site had the same snappy graphics, constantly updated news releases, and downloadable audio and video clips as other well-designed campaign sites, but it also included an interactive twist that showed that Mark Warner, more than almost any other candidate in the 1996 elections, understood the potential of the Net in a political context. In the corner of the site devoted to signing up campaign volunteers, supporters were asked to send the campaign headquarters e-mail if they heard, saw, or read of John W. Warner making an attack against Mark Warner that the Mark Warner campaign didn't rebut within twenty-four hours.

While this may not sound like much, consider that a number of other candidates across the country were paying consultants hundreds of thousands of dollars to monitor their opponents' every word, and respond to attacks within the twenty-four-hour "news cycle." By asking his supporters to alert his aides to attacks via the Net, Mark Warner "saved a bundle of money and developed a priceless new network of interested and informed voters at the same time," a former campaign consultant who didn't want to be identified told me.

Of course, no matter how futuristic some uses of political Web sites in 1996 were, other uses harkened back to time-honored mudslinging tactics. In August, Democrat James Martin Davis accused incumbent Rep. Jon Christensen, R-Nebr., of maintaining a campaign site that was only "five clicks" away from hard-core male pornography. Davis even called a press conference in Omaha to complain that Christensen's Web site made pictures from a male porn video called Capital Assets "easily accessible" to anyone with a computer. Christensen took his Web site down for a couple of weeks until the furor over Davis' charge died down; later Christensen beat Davis 57-43 percent.

For all their absurdity, Net-based spats like that in Nebraska mean "people are taking these new technologies seriously," Douglas Gomery, a University of Maryland professor who follows the economics of the Internet, said. "Nobody would have fought over something like this in 1992 because the Internet didn't matter much then."

Online Users and Losers in 1996

In 1994, about forty local, state, and congressional candidates nationwide had e-mail addresses, and no more than a handful of candidates for governorships and congressional seats put up Web sites. In 1996, those figures changed dramatically. More than 170 state and local candidates nationwide used the Web, according to one count. In another count, the California Voter Foundation tracked almost 300 campaign sites in California alone. At least one or two congressional candidates in every state had a Web presence; most states also had local and state candidate home pages. Eleven states—Alaska, Hawaii, Iowa, Louisiana, Maine, Mississippi, Nebraska, Nevada, Rhode Island, South Dakota, and Wyoming—didn't have local or state candidates on the Net, however. In largely rural states, or in states where the concentration of home computers and/or office-based Internet connections is small, most local and state candidates decided to save their meager campaign funds for television advertising instead.

Those 1996 candidates who put some of their funds into Web pages, however, considered the Net "a way to get unfiltered information out to the public, where they can act as a kind of truth squad in responding to an opponent's charges," said Colleen T. White, director of federal and state programs for Highway 1, a nonprofit organization founded in 1995 by five major computer software and hardware makers to help introduce Congress to the wonders of computerized communications.

While Alaska and Hawaii couldn't boast any Web sites for local candidates, they were at the forefront of innovative computerized communications on Election Night. Both of those states and nine others—Arizona, California, Delaware, Kansas, Kentucky, Missouri, New Mexico, Oklahoma, and South Carolina—provided live vote counts on every race from the local school board to the presidency via the Internet. The Net-based vote counts in all eleven states first went up on the Net two hours after the polls closed and were updated every fifteen minutes through the wee hours of the morning, according to a report by the Associated Press.

Why was there such a vast difference between the 1994 and 1996 campaigns when it came to the Net? Simple: Many voters wanted political information online. AT&T WorldNet Service, AT&T Corp.'s Internet access division, found in a survey conducted in mid-1996 that more than 65 percent of the voters they contacted were interested in using the Internet to find out where candidates stood on the issues. Almost a third of the people surveyed also said either that they would follow the coming elections on the Net, or that they would do so if they were able to access the Internet from work or home, AT&T WorldNet reported.

Of course, the most publicized Net campaigners were the Republican and Democratic candidates for president. Former Senator Robert Dole of Kansas broke ground for future campaign strategists by putting up a highly advanced campaign Web site in September 1995, some fifteen months before Election Day. His Web site offered audio clips, a volunteer signup-by-e-mail section, and downloadable screen savers featuring the candidate standing proudly in front of an American flag. In August 1996, the Dole campaign reworked its Web site to include short films of Dole making speeches and listings of the Republican nominee's campaign stops in every state.

The Clinton-Gore '96 Web site included several of the same offerings, but it didn't go up on the Net until almost ten months after the Dole Web site appeared. Sources close to the campaign suggested that the delay was due to strong opposition to a campaign Web site from Dick Morris, President Clinton's political advisor. Morris subsequently left the White House in the wake of a sex scandal.

Most campaign Web sites in 1996 got themselves into difficulty as well by relying on the same old material that campaigns have traditionally handed out in print form—speeches, photographs, position papers, sound bites, news releases, and clips from broadcast coverage and made-for-the-campaign documentaries. Some sites went further, adding interactive forms for voter comments on the campaign and e-mail for questions to the candidate. A few campaign sites even verged on tapping the true interactive power of the Net by asking supporters to be on guard for and notify the campaign of an opponent's claims (as Mark Warner's site did) or by adding moving headlines that updated supporters on the campaign's progress (as California Democrat Walter A. Capps's site did).

But too many campaign managers in 1996 seemed to think the Internet was nothing more than television on a computer screen. They offered voters information but didn't solicit feedback in return. As enamored as they were of computer technology, most political strategists in this election didn't know how to use the Net to persuade. For example, even the Dole and Clinton campaigns used student interns to answer e-mail, according to Heather Irwin, a political reporter for Hotwired. "People had this assumption that through e-mail they would be able to speak directly to the candidate or at least the candidate's office," Irwin told the AP. "But e-mail is just being printed out and put in the same pile with the snail mail. There really is no new kind of democracy coming out of this."

What Worked, What Didn't, and Why

Surveys that found that Americans wanted political information online were proven accurate on Election Night—maybe even too accurate. PoliticsNow, a political Web site operated by the *Washington Post*, ABC News, *Newsweek* magazine, the *Los Angeles Times*, and *National Journal*, went down for twenty minutes shortly after the first election results started pouring in. The stoppage occurred because UUNet Technologies Inc., the site's Internet service provider, suffered a "brownout" when thousands of Net users began logging in all at once to find out how their favorite candidates had fared at the polls.

Service on other sites lagged for up to ten minutes because of the overload from Net users seeking election results. AllPolitics, CNN's political Web site, had an estimated fifty million "hits" on Election Night, according to a report in the *Washington Post.* The closest AllPolitics had come to that sort of user demand had been two months earlier, when the combination of Hurricane Fran on the East Coast and a U.S. missile attack on Iraq prompted some eighteen million hits on the site.

Not that the 1996 election was a stellar one by any means. Pundits labeled the presidential campaign "boring" and voter turnout was off by anywhere from 3-38 percent at polling places across the country. In fact, one of the few really striking statistics to come out of the exit polls conducted by the Voter News Service with 70,000 voters nationwide was the fact that 26 percent of those voters called themselves "regular" users of the Internet.

In the weeks after the election, more startling figures appeared on the impact of Net-based information on voter choice in 1996. A survey released shortly after the election by Goddard*Clausen/First Tuesday, a Sacramento, California-based public affairs firm, found that almost one million California voters used their computers to gather political information before they went to the polls. A day later Wirthlin Worldwide, a McLean, Virginia-based political research firm, released a poll that reported that nine percent of American voters, or about 8.5 million people nationwide, said the information they found on the Internet influenced the way they voted. And in late December, the esteemed Pew Research Center for the People and the Press reported that 12 percent of the more than 1,000 adults the center had surveyed around Election Day said they used the Internet to obtain political information during the campaign. Significantly, three percent of the voters in the Pew survey said the computer was their principal source of election news.

Demand from Internet users who came to Walter Capps's site prompted Kenneth Owens, the site's Webmaster, to post a statement of his candidate's views that was far more detailed than similar Net-based candidate statements. Net users want more than mindless campaign commercials, Owens said. "In television, you've only got about thirty seconds to make your point," he told me. "What's different about the Net is that folks online aren't looking for a handbill or a thirty-second attack ad. They're doing research. They want and demand detailed content."

On the other hand, some political Web sites were embarrassingly clumsy. The California Republican Party's Web site, for example, opened in mid-October 1996 with biographies of state Democratic bigwigs but little information on the Republican candidates for state office, according to the *San Francisco Chronicle*. And McCracken (Ken) Poston, a Democrat running for Congress in North Georgia, tried to hold a "town hall meeting" in virtual reality on his Web site, but ran into a VR meltdown when a "heckler" in the shape of a B-1 bomber flew back and forth across the screen making outrageous comments. (Representative Nathan J. Deal, a Republican, beat Poston by a whopping 65–35 percent.)

The Internet and National Politics in the 1996 Campaigns

Campaign strategists weren't of one mind in assessing the impact of computer technology on the 1996 election cycle. Veteran political consultants—especially those who had weathered decades of campaign battles fought door-to-door in the precincts, from the podium at rallies, and through TV ads and Op-Ed pages—maintained that computers would never be a match for experience and traditional ward-heeling savvy. The older generation of consultants "say these gizmos aren't relevant, they're short-lived," J. Steven Wagner, the head of QEV Analytics Ltd., a Washington-based consulting firm, said.

Much of the consultants' skepticism stemmed from the poor record companies attempting to sell services through the Web had compiled by 1996. Net users resisted paying for political information then, just as they do today. For example, *Slate* magazine, the acclaimed e-zine of political analysis founded by Microsoft Corp. and edited by veteran political commentator Michael Kinsley, announced in early 1996 that it was dropping plans to charge subscription fees because the editors had concluded that Netizens still aren't willing to pay extra for specific content. "Pornographic and financial sites are a possible exception," Kinsley wrote. "But even in our headiest moments, we couldn't convince ourselves that people lust for political and cultural commentary the way they lust for sex or money."

Some political consultants cautioned, however, that the Internet shouldn't have been expected to deliver all the benefits that the overblown hype promised. "The bottom line in 1996 is that probably no one is going to say, 'I won or lost the election because of the Internet,'" Phil Noble, president of Phil Noble & Associates, a Charleston, South Carolina-based political consulting firm, said. "But I think this will be the last election where that will happen."

The 1998 Campaign Online

The Good News: More, More, More

Conventional political wisdom says that everything really interesting happens during presidential elections—and that no one cares all that much about mid-term elections. But contrary to the conventional wisdom, 1998 was a remarkable election year for the Net.

First, there were far more candidates online than there had been two years earlier. Of the 1,296 candidates who ran for Congress or for governor in the 1998 election, 43 percent used the Web, Elaine C. Karmack, executive director of Visions of Governance for the Twenty-First Century, a research program at the John F. Kennedy School of Government of Harvard University, reported in her recent study, "Campaigning on the Internet in the Off-Year Elections of 1998." Other surveys estimated that, compared to 1996, the number of candidates for local, state, and federal office who had Web sites increased 60 percent by 1998.

Some political consultants even boasted that they had created entire political campaigns online in 1998. Barbara Bode, a Washington-based consultant, told an audience at a panel discussion sponsored by the Freedom Forum shortly before Election Day that her online campaigns had even included newsletters and get-out-the-vote information via e-mail. The Internet is "a very powerful, very intimate medium," Bode said. "The real effort is to get more and more low-income (people) online who are now online illiterate."

Studies conducted before and after the 1998 election also showed that more voters than ever before were going online to search for political information. In California, for example, 45 percent of the state's voters were Internet users, the *Los Angeles Times* reported. The Pew Research Center for the People and the Press found—in a study conducted from October through early December, 1998—that 16 percent of the voting population in the United States gathered information about the election from the Internet. Only 10 percent of U.S. voters had gone to the Net for information two years earlier. Even more noteworthy, the number of voters who considered the Internet their primary source of election information doubled in 1998, to 6 percent from the 3 percent recorded in exit polls two years earlier, Pew reported.

Online coverage of political news expanded in 1998 to meet the increased demand for election information. ABC News's online coverage on Election Night, for example, included results in gubernatorial and congressional races, and "live chats" with reporters, election analysts, and the winners and losers in contests across the country. At the same time, the number of Net users who flocked to election-related Web sites in the waning days of the campaign exceeded even the most optimistic expectations, the *New York Times* reported. Traffic at the California Voter Foundation site during the last weekend before the election increased to twenty-eight times the normal rate, while the number of users in America Online's election area was double the amount predicted, according to the *Times*.

Of course, by 1998 more Americans than ever before were exploring the Internet for a variety of reasons, and that certainly accounted for some of the booming interest in election information. The percentage of U.S. adults using the Net had risen from 15 percent in 1995 to about 41 percent in 1998, and almost half of those people had gone online for the first time in the past year, the Pew study reported. More important, by 1998 anywhere from one-sixth to one quarter of *all* U.S. adults—not just regular Internet users—were checking online sites for news at least once a week, the study found.

Amidst all the hype about the public's interest in following the campaigns online, however, one set of findings signaled a profound change in the Internet's impact on politics. In 1998, Americans began to turn to the Internet for help in deciding how to cast their votes.

More than half of the users of the *New York Times*'s Web site said that they would go to the Internet if they were undecided about whom to vote for, a study conducted for the New York Times Electronic Media Co. reported a month after the election. In the Pew study, one-third of the regular Net users surveyed said that what they found online influenced their vote.

A Dearth of Dialogue

That was the good news about online campaigning in 1998. Unfortunately, most candidates, Republican, Democrat, and independent alike, squandered the advantage the Net handed them.

In general, candidates in 1998 continued to use the Web like a campaign brochure. Net users could find basic biographical information on the candidate and at least a few statements of his or her position on key issues, but that was about it. Some sites added news updates on the candidate, or copies of stump speeches, or even pictures from the campaign trail, but there was little of the give-and-take that makes the Internet so vibrant—and so radically different from the traditional media.

In her study of online campaigns, for example, Elaine Karmack found that less than one-fifth of the sites she and her associates studied were updated regularly, and only a handful encouraged Net users to "cyber-volunteer" by sending friends electronic postcards supporting the candidate or by downloading and printing out bumper stickers. Only two sites out of the 554 studied were "fully interactive," meaning that they offered visitors the ability to "engage in a dialogue with the candidate or the campaign."

Why, when American voters were rushing to the Net in their eagerness to engage with and support a candidate, were politicians themselves so unwilling to respond? Fear, Karmack suggests. "Control of the message is as much a campaign obsession as is money, and one explanation is that candidates fear losing control of the message," she wrote. "But entering into an online discussion with voters is no different than appearing on a radio call-in show or showing up at an open meeting—things which candidates regularly do—and where they are regularly subjected to difficult and sometimes embarrassing questions."

Along Comes Jesse

One campaign in 1998 figuratively (and, sometimes, literally) tossed out all the conventional wisdom, however, and showed that the interactivity of the Internet could provide the winning margin.

When Jesse Ventura, a former professional wrestler, set out early in the year to seek the governorship of Minnesota on the Reform Party ticket, political insiders snickered. Not only was Ventura a rank political neophyte but also the Reform Party was only six years old. There was no party infrastructure within Minnesota, no established network of leaders, organizers, and volunteers in the state to roust out the vote come November. Ventura didn't even have a campaign headquarters.

Phil Madsen, a software instructor who had been active in the petition drive to put Ross Perot on the Minnesota ballot in 1992, volunteered to set up a Web site for the Ventura campaign. Madsen admits that he had never created a Web site before. "I figured this was as good a time as any to learn how to do it, so I bought Microsoft FrontPage 98, found a Web site host that charged $30 a month, and went to work," he said at the annual Politics Online conference at George Washington University, in Washington, a month after Ventura stunned the national political establishment by winning the Minnesota race.

That win—by an unknown candidate with a colorful history, backed only by a handful of third-party enthusiasts armed with cell phones, home fax machines, a Web site, and e-mail accounts—has caused an enormous amount of controversy among the campaign cognoscenti. Did Ventura prevail because of the Internet? Or because of other factors such as voter apathy or anger? Was his election a fluke? Or a harbinger of things to come as the Information Age begins to flower?

Whatever the political scientists conclude, it's worth noting the ways in which the Ventura campaign drew upon the unique characteristics of the online medium to fill in the gaps caused by a lack of money and manpower:

- **Jesse Net**—Madsen created a page on the Ventura Web site where supporters could register their e-mail addresses and be added to an online mailing list. By Election Day, Madsen said, the mailing list had 3,000 names. The Ventura campaign worked the list heavily, using it to raise both money and volunteers. When the campaign found itself short of volunteers for a booth at the Minnesota State Fair, for example, a plea went out on the Jesse Net and the problem was solved. "In the old days, we used to call people on the telephone one at a time to raise volunteers. Now we can raise them by the dozens with a single e-mail message," Madsen said.

- **Online fundraising**—Over $50,000 of the almost $174,000 raised by the Ventura campaign came from online contributions made through the Web site or Jesse Net, Madsen said. In addition, the campaign solicited guaranteed bank loans from supporters via the Internet.
- **Technology-expedited communications and data entry**—The Ventura campaign held few staff meetings, "but we were in constant communication with each other via cell phones and the Internet," Madsen said. When 5,000 people filled out forms at the State Fair requesting further information on the Ventura campaign, volunteers working on their own PCs at home entered the new names and addresses in a campaign database via the Web site.
- **"Get-Out-The-Vote" tactics based on the Internet**—The most striking element of the Ventura campaign was its use of electronic communications to rally supporters almost instantaneously throughout the state. Two weeks before Election Day the campaign took off in a caravan of motor homes for a tour of Minnesota, stopping every hour or so during the day for a rally. The Internet and cell phones became the campaign's lifeline. "The caravan often fell behind schedule," Madsen has written in a memo about the campaign published on the Net. "One person in the caravan was in constant touch with another back home who was updating the Web site every few minutes with reports about the caravan's progress. In towns where crowds were waiting, someone in the crowd was usually in touch by cell phone or runner with someone at home who was tracking the caravan's progress on the Web site. Even though we were quite late at times, the crowds held because they knew exactly where we were, why we were late, and when to expect us." This system worked so well that a hastily called rally at 10 p.m. on a Sunday night in Hutchison, Minnesota, drew some 600 supporters, and almost 700 supporters showed up at a rally an hour later in Willmar, not far down the road, according to the *St. Paul Pioneer Press*.

Madsen has been widely quoted as saying, "While it's true that we could not have won the election without the Internet, we did not win the election because of the Internet." He's right, because campaigns are won or lost not on the basis of one innovation in politicking but on a combination of good techniques, fortuitous events, and simple luck. But that doesn't mean that the Ventura campaign's Internet strategies should be discounted.

Dan Lungren, who was running for governor of California, and Jeb Bush, who campaigned for (and won) the governorship of Florida, also discovered that e-mail could be a valuable tool for reaching out to supporters and mobilizing volunteers. Lungren established a 1,500-member mailing list during his campaign, while Jeb Bush corresponded regularly via e-mail with over 1,000 supporters who had joined his mailing list via his Web site. Sen. Barbara Boxer, D-Calif., who was running for re-election in 1998, not only raised more than $25,000 through her Web site, but also organized a series of neighborhood-based "Boxer House Parties" through her 673 online volunteers. Two other innovations on the Boxer Web site—a fundraising concert presented online, and the sale of "Boxer Shorts"—are likely to be widely imitated in coming campaigns.

Did these online devices attract votes? It depends on who's talking. Rick Alber, the lawyer-turned-software-designer who developed the Boxer Web site, estimates that the online campaign contributed almost 11 percent of the votes that sent Boxer back to the Senate for a second term. Rufus N. Montgomery, Jr., who designed the Jeb Bush Web site, isn't so sure. "I think our e-mail lists were helpful in keeping track of our volunteers and supporters, but I'd hesitate to say the Web site actually won votes," he said during a panel presentation at the Politics Online conference.

From the looks of the 1996 and 1998 campaigns, the Internet's defining moment in American politics had yet to arrive. The question everyone began asking was "What will the millennium bring?"

Chapter 9

Election 2000 ... and Counting

Due to the recent ballot confusion in Florida the Presidential election process has been cancelled for this term ... It has now been granted to the common citizen the chance to be President. ... At the end of the auction the high bidder will be flown in to Washington, D.C., to prepare for inauguration ceremonies and [be] prepped for presidential duty.

—Description for Item No. 497945868, the job of forty-third president of the United States, which went up for bid on the online auction site eBay around 9:50 A.M. Pacific Standard Time on November 13, 2000. The opening bid was one penny, but the price soared to $100 million before eBay closed the auction down some four hours later.

In terms of politics and the Internet, Election 2000 was a paradox. More candidates raised money, more Americans searched for political news, and more campaign organizing occurred online in 2000 than ever before. At the same time, not since the advent of the World Wide Web a decade ago have technology issues meant so little in the presidential campaign—or have efforts to draw voters to commercial political Web sites met with so little success.

Yet neither the 2000 election nor the Internet's role in it will be remembered for dollars raised, volunteers recruited or issues debated, online or offline. Instead, Election 2000 will be known for the national nightmare that ensued when no clear victor emerged in the presidential race in Florida on November 7. In the wake of the Florida recount battle "electronic voting" became the rallying cry for Americans who believe computers can prevent a similar fiasco in the future.

It's the Technology, Stupid!

The first inkling of trouble in Florida came excruciatingly early in the morning the day after the polls closed on November 7. Around 2:20 A.M. Eastern Standard Time on November 8 most of the major television networks took early poll results that seemed to put the state in Texas Governor George W. Bush's camp, and called the presidential race for him. Winning Florida would give Bush 271 electoral college votes—one more than he needed to be elected—CNN, NBC, CBS, and ABC announced. Only a few hours later, however, the networks retracted their calls. As the Florida tallies mounted through the night the margin between Bush and Vice President Al Gore never grew larger than one-half of 1 percent. Under Florida law, any time the final margin between candidates in a statewide election is that small, election officials are automatically required to recount the votes.

In the days that followed, controversy mounted over the layout of ballots themselves. In Palm Beach County, for example, elections supervisor Theresa Le Pore had designed a punch card ballot with a "butterfly" design listing on two facing pages the ten candidates in the presidential race eligible to be on the ballot in Florida. Punch holes for each name ran down the middle of the lists. While each name was marked with an arrow that pointed to a hole, voters complained that that it was difficult to discern which hole was the right one when they slid the ballots into a metal punch mechanism to mark the candidate of their choice. Those complaints added to election officials' concern when it was discovered that some 19,000 Palm Beach ballots contained "over-votes," or votes for more than one presidential candidate. Also, after the polls closed, Reform Party candidate Patrick J. Buchanan had won 3,407 votes—a startling number given the 337 registered Reform Party voters in Palm

Beach County. Since Buchanan's name fell in between Bush's and Gore's names on the ballot, Democratic poll watchers argued that the "butterfly" design had caused Gore voters to punch the hole for Buchanan by mistake.

By the Friday following the election, Gore's advisers had called for a hand recount of contested ballots in four Florida counties: Palm Beach, Miami-Dade, Broward (which includes Ft. Lauderdale), and Volusia (home to Daytona Beach). Election officials hastily gathered teams of employees and Democratic and Republican party representatives, and the laborious recount process began.

In its own way, technology dictated the decision to hand-count the ballots rather than simply running them through a counter again. In Palm Beach, as in 20 percent of Florida counties, for example, voters cast their votes using a VotoMatic machine, which punches small, perforated rectangles out of heavy paper cards modeled after the cards IBM used in its mainframe computers in the 1960s. Punching a rectangle out cleanly, so that it's no longer attached to the card, can be tricky, however. And ascertaining the voter's intent when the rectangle, or "chad," still clings to the ballot, can be trickier still. As the recount wore on, a new lexicon of terms hit the front pages and nightly newscasts across the United States. Was a chad "hanging"—meaning attached by only one corner, indicating the voter made a clear attempt to punch through—or merely "dimpled"—meaning that it bulged slightly, indicating that the voter probably didn't mean to punch there? The worst cases were the "pregnant" chads, where the rectangle was clearly dented but had not broken through. Did the dent indicate that the voter had meant to punch out the rectangle and register a vote but had perhaps not punched hard enough? Or could it be that the voter had started to punch and then changed his or her mind?

Meanwhile, an army of lawyers and political operatives from both the Bush and Gore camps argued the validity of the recount through the courts. At first, Florida Secretary of State Katherine Harris ruled that the recounts had to be completed by November 14, seven days after the election. The Florida Supreme Court overruled Harris, however, and extended the recount until Sunday, November 26. By that time, the U.S. Supreme Court had stepped into the fray. Both the Florida Supreme Court and the U.S. Supreme Court again weighed in on the question of whether the recounts should continue. The Florida court said yes on December 8, and the High Court said no the next day.

Finally, on December 12, after hearing lengthy arguments from both sides, the U.S. Supreme Court issued a five to four decision that brought additional recounts in Florida to a halt. Gore conceded on December 13. While he had captured the popular vote by 539,897 votes, Bush had prevailed in the Electoral College.

As the recount saga played out in the "old" media, millions of Americans also followed it on the Internet. On Election Day, for example, 12 percent of Americans went online for political news, the Pew Research Center reported. The very next day, that number jumped to 18 percent. Two weeks later, when the Florida Supreme Court posted its ruling extending the recount in a PDF file on the Web, almost as many people rushed to download it as had downloaded the Starr Report two years earlier, according to the online news service Newsbytes.

Meanwhile, e-mail and message boards became potent weapons in the public relations war Bush and Gore backers fought outside the Florida courtrooms. "Contribute now. The expense of the recount effort must be funded immediately," Bush supporters urged in a message sent the week after the election to the hundreds of thousands of e-mail addresses the GOP had gathered during the presidential campaign. Some Internet users set up Web sites to express their perspectives on the recount, while others made do with postings on sites with already-established traffic. "Gore, go away. The GOP now controls the Presidency, the House, the Senate, and the U.S. Supreme Court," another Bush supporter wrote on CNN.com.

In one case, the online furor over the recount even threatened to clog up the works in the inboxes of leading U.S. newspapers. According to a report in the *Boston Globe*, Joseph A. Morris, the outgoing president of the United Republican Fund of Illinois, sent an e-mail to friends two days after the election urging them to "bombard the news media and our public officials" with electronic messages if Gore did not concede immediately. "If it becomes widely reported—and it will—that there is a groundswell demanding that Gore back down and not embarrass the country, he will have to relent," the message said. A week later anti-Gore e-mails were pouring into editorial page inboxes at the *Chicago Sun Times*, the *Washington Post*, the *Los Angeles Times*, the *New York*

Post, the *New York Times*, and the *Globe* itself at the rate of almost 1,000 messages a day. "I have learned a lesson," Morris told the *Globe* when the newspaper reached him via telephone. "I had no idea about the power of the medium."

But technophiles did. And as the recount saga finally came to a close, the debate over computer-based voting took on a new urgency, with proponents insisting it would be the best way to avoid "another Palm Beach."

The debate quickly divided into two convergent camps. The first, which included a number of public policy analysts and some technical experts, argued that the addition of computer technology to traditional voting machines would be sufficient to overcome the problems associated with the Florida recount. Ironically, in its decision halting those very recounts, the U.S. Supreme Court alluded to this argument. "This case has shown that punch card balloting machines can produce an unfortunate number of ballots which are not punched in a clean, complete way by the voter," the High Court noted. "After the current counting, it is likely legislative bodies nationwide will examine ways to improve the mechanisms and machinery for voting."

The second camp, however, wanted to go much farther, arguing that it is time to begin a national exploration into an Internet-based voting system. Tech-savvy Americans would welcome this option, they argued. Indeed, in a poll taken a month after the election, the Gartner Group, a well-respected research firm, found that one-third of Americans would be willing to use the Internet, or e-mail, to register to vote, request an absentee ballot, and cast a vote.

But both camps had plenty of detractors, particularly among those experts who feared that the glitches inherent in what is still an evolving technical field would frighten American voters far more than had the "Spectacle of the Chads."

Whether computerized voting technology involves upgrades to traditional voting machines or a paradigm shift to a fully Internet-based system, the debate that followed the election highlighted both the technology's strengths and weaknesses.

Of the over 140 million registered voters in the United States, for example, only approximately 9 percent currently vote on computerized ATM-like machines that use touch-sensitive screens. The great advantage of these "direct recording electronic devices," or DREs for short, is that they prohibit a voter from choosing more candidates than there are positions available. If touch-screen machines had been used in Palm Beach, proponents say, there would have been no computerized equivalent of the over-vote. Also, touch-screen machines offer the voter the opportunity to review the entire ballot before pressing a button that directs the machine's computer to tally the votes and send them electronically to a central location, meaning that there would have been no question of whether voters meant to vote for Buchanan or Gore.

Even though the touch-screen machines are little more than electronic versions of the old-fashioned lever machines first used in the United States in the nineteenth century, supporters say their computerized capabilities not only reduce costs—by eliminating the need for precinct workers to record tallies manually when the polls close—but also dramatically speed up the reporting process—which helps stave off hasty vote projections by news organizations unwilling to wait for the slower process of counting punch-card ballots.

Touch-screen machines are also gaining acceptance in other industrialized countries. Some 80 percent of the precincts in the Netherlands now use a form of computerized voting technology. Brazil first used touch-screen electronic voting machines in selected 1996 municipal elections; in Election 2000 every Brazilian voted via DREs.

But there's a catch: Touch-screen machines cost from $3,000 to $7,000 each, and even small precincts in the United States would need at least two DREs to accommodate voters, American election officials say. Riverside County, California, which replaced its outmoded voting technology in 2000, reportedly paid $14 million for 4,250 touch-screen machines. Philadelphia, which will replace its system in 2001, is spending $17 million. The National Association of State Election Directors has estimated that it would cost between $4.2 billion and $6.5 billion to replace older voting technology nationwide with the touch-screen systems. Those sums are far more than most of the 175,000 voting precincts in the country—many of them financially strapped—can afford.

Also, unlike the old-fashioned lever machine that registered each vote on a mechanical counter at the back of the machine, a DRE that fails either to record a vote or to record it accurately leaves no record to re-check after the fact. As electronic voting expert Lorrie Faith Cranor has noted, when the polls closed on Election Day 2000 in Roosevelt County, New Mexico, officials discovered that 533 absentee ballots hadn't been properly counted. Since the votes had been recorded on "optically scanned ballots," meaning that voters marked their choices by darkening a small circle next to the name of the candidate, much like on a standardized test, the scanner that had made the miscount was repaired and the votes recounted. "Without physical ballots to rescan, it might not have been possible to correct this problem," Cranor wrote in a posting to "e-lection," an open mailing list she operates to address electronic voting issues.

Given the problems inherent in any stand-alone voting machine, Internet-based voting is a much more cost-effective and efficient option, other technologists argue. An online system would free voters not only from the physical limitations of paper ballots—online ballots could be used at home, in the voter's native language if necessary, and in a wide range of type sizes—but also from the fear that their choices might not be reported accurately. Systems could be designed with "help" pages to walk voters through the online process, print-out functions so that voters could review their choices in a paper format, and double, triple, even quadruple electronic reminders that would ask voters "Are you sure this is what you want?" before they press the "send" button.

Even the threat of hackers, computer viruses, and denial-of-service attacks are overrated, some Internet voting proponents say. A week before Election Day, for example, San Rafael, California-based Safevote Inc. conducted a mock online election in Contra Costa County, California, and invited the Net community to try to compromise it. In an attempt to make potential mischief-makers' jobs easy, Safevote posted the system's network protocols and its software, hardware, and data formats on the company Web page. Nothing happened—except that 307 voters stopped by the county election offices in Martinez, California, to try the system out. "More tests are needed before Internet voting can replace even what we have in Florida, but Safevote's official test in Contra Costa shows that a system can be designed such that election results depend on voter's choices, not lack of choices," company CEO Ed Gerck wrote in a posting to "e-lection."

Other online voting experiments in California on or before Election Day 2000 also drew enthusiastic responses from voters, according to the companies that conducted the experiments. All of the voters who tried online voting from computers set up by VoteHere.net in polling places in San Diego and Sacramento counties found the systems "easy or very easy to use," and 65 percent of those polled also said they would vote from home via the Internet if they believed their votes would be secure, the *New York Times* reported. And when Kids Voting, a national nonprofit organization, staged an online voting experiment for more than 6,000 children in thirty-three California schools the week of the election, the project went so smoothly that Paul Doscher, vice president of Entrust Technologies Inc., which provided the security software, told the *San Jose Mercury News* that "had grown-ups used the same kind of system, what happened in Palm Beach could never happen."

Perhaps the most telling testimonial to the power of online voting to come out of Election 2000, however, originated in Okaloosa County, Florida, where a handful of the votes generated through the Department of Defense's online voting experiment were tallied. When CNet News asked her opinion of the experiment, county supervisor of elections Pat Hollarn replied, "I long for the day when we can do this across the board."

But the same issues that have always plagued proposals for Internet voting systems still exist, critics note. During the Arizona Democratic primary, for example, civil rights groups traveled to rural and inner-city areas with laptops to ensure that the voters there could participate. What would happen to voters such as these if an Internet voting system were to be established nationwide? As one journalist touting Internet voting noted, Americans "who are sick, traveling, or just too busy, for example, could easily cast their votes from home, work, a hotel room, or even the back of a taxi cab with a wireless device." But what about those citizens who aren't wired?

Critics also insist that online voting isn't as easy as shopping or banking on the Web. In an interview with the *Washington Post* following the election, David Jefferson, the chairman of the California task force on Internet voting, argued that security issues for voting are much harder to resolve than they are for financial transactions, where both sides know all the details of the transaction and can easily get a paper copy as proof that the transaction took place. "In a vote, both parties don't have complete information. If they [voters] know that they cast a fraudulent vote, they can't go in and remove it," Jefferson said.

In fact, the prospect of widespread Internet voting so alarmed a panel of technology experts and social scientists convened by the National Science Foundation that they warned strongly against implementing it in a report released in early March 2001. "The security risks associated with these systems are both numerous and pervasive, and in many cases cannot be resolved using even the most sophisticated technology today," the panel, which included noted academics from MIT, Caltech, Yale, and the University of California at Berkeley, as well as Cranor and Jefferson, wrote in *Report of the National Workshop on Internet Voting: Issues and Research Agenda.* "In addition, many of the social science concerns regarding the effects of remote voting on the electoral process would need to be addressed before any such system could be responsibly deployed."

But proponents of online voting maintain that casting a ballot via the Internet will be an option sooner rather than later. VoteHere, for example, reportedly expected to win approval for its systems in as many as forty states in 2000. Meta Group, a research firm, has estimated that it would cost $250 million to build a national Web-based voting system that could process votes nationwide within the fifteen-hour period now set aside for federal elections. While some technical experts disagree with Meta Group's prediction that one system could handle a traffic volume that would include up to ten pages of local, state, and national vote data from each voter and could run as high as 13.6 million electronic votes per hour, no one has suggested that such a system itself is unattainable. Like the famous phrase that Clinton backers repeated over and over in the 1992 presidential campaign—"It's the economy, stupid!"—online voting supporters believe voting problems can be solved if the country will only focus on technology first and foremost.

Did the Internet Really Matter This Time?

Other than renewing the debate over computerized or Internet-based voting technology, the Internet had only mixed success in

Election 2000. Fundraising via the Web skyrocketed, and campaigns across the country finally discovered how to use e-mail to get their messages out to potential voters and the news media. Counterbalancing those successes, however, were the growing concerns over privacy and Internet-aided vote swapping. Plus, in many ways, neither the presidential candidates nor voters themselves seemed particularly energized by—or even interested in—Internet issues.

Fundraising Scored Big

First the good news: Online fundraising worked better than even the most enthusiastic online politicos had imagined it would. By the time he dropped out of the race in early March, Republican John McCain reportedly garnered more than $6.4 million in total online donations to his campaign. Former Sen. Bill Bradley, a contender in the Democratic presidential primaries, raised $2 million—8 percent of his total donations—online. MoveOn.org, the Web-based organization that began as an effort to convince Congress to drop the impeachment of President Clinton, raised $2.25 million online in 2000 and passed that money on to some thirty candidates in nationwide races, according to the *San Francisco Chronicle*. Over 90 percent of those who contributed online to MoveOn.org gave $50 or less.

Figures like these are sure to gladden the heart of cash-strapped campaigns and activist groups dependent on fundraising for their operating expenses. Direct mail operations typically take forty to fifty cents out of every dollar they raise, and rarely achieve better than a 1 percent "return rate," or one donation for every 100 letters mailed. Telemarketers take as much as seventy cents per dollar and achieve similarly low rates of return. Candidates in 2000 raised as much as $10 million online, PoliticsOnline, a well-regarded political Web site, has estimated; that figure could go as high as $20 million when all accounts are in. Given the cost-efficient nature of online fundraising, much of that money goes directly into the pockets of the people or organizations for which it is intended.

Organizing at Cyberspeed

Also, after fumbling around for years, political operatives finally learned in Election 2000 how to put the communications power of the Internet to work—at least in one direction.

E-mail became the "killer app" for campaign managers eager to recruit and motivate volunteers. As the campaign season went into high gear in the summer of 2000, both the Democratic National Committee (DNC) and the Republican National Committee (RNC) initiated e-mail campaigns asking the online faithful to send party-generated e-mails to their friends, in an electronic version of the chain letter. "We believe electronic word-of-mouth is the best form of voter contact," Larry Purpuro, deputy chief of staff at the RNC and director of its "e.GOP" project, told the *New York Times*. "It's personalized, it's targeted, and it works with lightning speed." Both the Bush and Gore campaigns also established spread-the-word efforts via e-mail—Bush operatives labeled their mailing list the "Bush e-train," while Gore's Webmasters went their opponents one better, collecting instant-message "handles" from interested Netizens and transmitting action items and updates within seconds of publication.

Candidates at other levels also added e-mail organizing to their collection of campaign strategies. In addition to raising money online, the McCain campaign also recruited some 26,000 volunteers via e-mail outreach. On her campaign Web site Maria Cantwell, the Democratic candidate for (and later winner of) the state's open seat in the U.S. Senate, sponsored an e-mail discussion group called C2C, for "Cantwell to community," as well as linking supporters to online voter registration and absentee ballot sites.

Cantwell would be expected to be tech-savvy: She became a senior vice president at Seattle-based RealNetworks after she was defeated in her bid for re-election to the U.S. House of Representatives in 1994. But she wasn't alone in recognizing the value of this political version of "viral marketing," an old advertising technique that has gained prominence in the high-tech industry in recent years. In the consumer arena the aim of viral marketing is to transmit sales messages in as nonthreatening a fashion as possible, by putting "friends in touch with friends" who share the same interests and, theoretically, product needs. In the political realm, where voters are alert to any hint of coercion, viral marketing messages represent a softball approach to persuading others to consider a candidate's position and, it's hoped, support that position at the polls.

During the 2000 campaigns, however, these e-mail efforts ranged from the subtle to the shrill. Both the Bush and Gore camps, for example, sent daily messages about upcoming rallies, campaign events, and local political issues to the directors of community organizations, party volunteer coordinators, activists, and interest groups who would in turn e-mail the messages to their own lists of friends and colleagues. Normally the messages concentrated on generalized concerns, such as the environment, medical care for seniors, education, and tax cuts, or solicited volunteer help for voter registration drives and rallies on the candidates' whistle stops. But as Election Day neared, the tone of the messages became more strident. "PASS THIS E-MAIL ALONG AND HELP AL GORE WIN THE FIGHT!" by taking ten Gore supporters to the polls, an e-mail from the Gore campaign implored recipients, according to the *New York Times*. The message also included a list of the candidate's endorsements and a link to a page on his campaign Web site where Netizens could design personalized pro-Gore sites of their own and distribute links to them in similar rounds of e-mail. The GOP engaged in quieter but equally impassioned language. Two days before voters were due to go to the polls, a message bearing the name of no less a personage than former Joint Chiefs of Staff chairman (and now Secretary of State) Colin Powell went out to more than 900,000 Republicans urging them to "help elect our Republican team." The volume of these last-ditch messages hit mammoth proportions in the final ten days of the presidential campaign, with e-mails reportedly distributed to as many as twenty to thirty million party members from both sides.

At the same time that e-mail propelled traditional grassroots organizing to cyberspeed in 2000, it was also being used to push the latest campaign message to an increasingly wired news media. Months before the Democrats and Republicans convened formally to anoint their presidential candidates, Bush and Gore aides pumped out an unremitting stream of position statements, press releases, proposals, speeches, and rapid-response factoids to e-mail lists containing the names of up to 2,000 reporters, editors, and producers. While most of the material had a legitimate political aim—to shape press coverage to the candidate's advantage, while throwing his opponent off balance—the sheer volume of it could be stunning. In less than twenty-four hours after the Bush campaign's release of a major economic plan in late September, for example, Bush and Gore operatives released a barrage of fifty-six e-mails aimed solely at influencing the way the news media interpreted the plan, the *Wall Street Journal* reported. Speed was essential to achieving the desired effect. "If they [Bush aides] put out a press release and it's unanswered by us, the reporter who has five minutes to file might think it's true," Gore aide David Ginsberg told the *Journal*.

As popular as e-mail became as an organizing and press relations tool in the 2000 campaigns, however, it only conveyed information one way: from the campaign headquarters outward. In an election where every vote counted and candidates were desperate to get supporters to the polls, e-mail clearly provided a low-cost, efficient way to rally the troops. But political campaigns have yet to learn how to use it to its full potential.

Trade-Offs Online

While online fundraising and e-mail-based organizing prospered, vote-swapping Web sites, another online political innovation in Election 2000, didn't do so well. But it wasn't for lack of imagination—or trying.

In late September, polls began to show longtime political activist and Green Party presidential candidate Ralph Nader nearing the 5 percent of the popular vote that he needed to get in order for the party to receive federal matching funds for a presidential campaign in 2004. At the same time, Gore's lead was slipping in a number of closely contested states, including the Electoral College heavy-hitters Michigan, Pennsylvania, and Florida. By early October, a Web site aptly named NaderTrader.org appeared, urging Nader supporters who lived in the battleground states to swap their votes via the Internet with Gore backers who lived in states such as Texas, Louisiana, Virginia, and Alaska, where a Bush victory was a foregone conclusion. Within days, seven similar Web sites sprang up.

By Election Day, organizers of the "Nader Trader" movement were estimating that 15,000 people had taken the vote-swapping pledge.

That wasn't enough. Nader didn't win the requisite 5 percent of the vote and Gore lost the presidency. Meanwhile, Voteswap2000 and Votexchange2000, two California-based sites, shut down just days before the election after learning that the California secretary of state was threatening to take legal action against them for violating a law against inducing a citizen of the state to vote one way or another.

Still, vote-swapping sites may have a future. The ACLU has filed a lawsuit in Los Angeles asking the federal courts to make the California secretary of state back down from his threats, according to CNet News. And, in a sure sign of confidence, Alan Porter, Webmaster for Votexchange2000, has already registered the domain name "Votexchange2004."

E-mail Lists Erode Privacy ...

Now for the bad news. The same lists of hundreds of thousands of e-mail addresses that gave political campaigns the wherewithal to mobilize supporters quickly during the 2000 election season were augmented by software and research methods that probed voters' personal lives to an unprecedented degree. What's more, using information that's either freely available via public records like automobile and property titles, voting records, and driver's license databanks or purchased from credit bureaus and other information vendors, campaigns were able to target both their online and offline messages not only according to voters' age, race, and gender but also to their lifestyles, income, and personal interests.

Did a campaign want to reach Democratic women age forty and over in the Northeast who had donated to environmental causes in the past five years? How about thirty to fifty-five-year-old Republican men who live in California and whose Web-surfing habits indicate they are concerned about healthcare? Or childless professionals on Chicago's Gold Coast whose names are on the membership records of groups opposed to bailing out Social Security? Not a problem, particularly if the campaign represented one of the forty-five senators, more than 200 members of the House or forty-six Republican and Democratic state parties that bought mailing lists from Aristotle International Inc., which has built a database of information on 150 million registered voters whose names and addresses the company gathered from local voter rolls across the nation.

Private firms weren't the only players in the voter information business, however. According to a remarkable story by *Washington Post* reporters John Mintz and Robert O'Harrow Jr., independent interest groups from both sides of the political spectrum also amass disparate information about voters and fashion profiles of nonmembers likely to be sympathetic to their causes. The National Rifle Association, for example, buys lists of pickup truck owners, people with hunting licenses, concealed weapons permit holders, gun show exhibitors, and outdoor magazine subscribers, and sorts the lists electronically to arrive at the names of potential allies, Mintz and O'Harrow reported. The National Abortion and Reproductive Rights Action League creates profiles of typical pro-choice women, based on the demographics of its own members, and then searches for nonmembers who visit the same Web sites, read the same newspapers, or listen to the same radio stations. "It scares the hell out of me," John Aravosis, an Internet consultant who advises clients about online marketing, was quoted as saying. "Political information is per se more sensitive. ... People have no clue about what these companies do."

Most important, invasions of voter privacy don't stop with the compilation of these lists. Visitors to a campaign Web site often voluntarily give their e-mail addresses so they can receive information about that specific candidate. But few voters on the Net realize the extent to which campaigns swap, rent, or even steal e-mail lists—and in the process make the names on the lists unwitting targets for spam.

In 1996, for example, the Dole campaign leased its e-mail lists to a handful of other Republican candidates in the final weeks before the election. Chagrined when a minor furor broke out over the practice, Dole aides quickly sent follow-up messages explaining the "unsubscribe" process in detail.

More recently, e-mail messages bearing the name of Thomas E. Bellanca, a contender for the Democratic nomination in the race for Virginia's 11th Congressional district, went out to portions of the massive e-mail database that had been amassed by the Bill Bradley campaign before Bradley withdrew from the presidential primary in

March 2000. "Dear Bill Bradley Supporters," the April 2 e-mail read. "It's not too late to keep the Bill Bradley vision alive. … In order to win, I need to get as many delegates that support issues that Bill Bradley took the leadership role in bringing to the forefront." When a series of postings protesting the Bellanca message appeared on "Politech," the popular politics-and-technology mailing list, Bradley Webmaster Lynn Reed insisted that the campaign hadn't authorized the use of its list. "Some volunteers had access to certain portions of our e-mail list during the campaign as part of their access to our supporter database … and it would have been possible for them to make a copy of the list, although they were instructed in print and verbally not to do so," Reed wrote.

But acknowledging the problem doesn't resolve it. Several weeks before she wrote to "Politech," Reed had told the audience at a seminar in Washington, D.C., that 85 percent of the hundreds of thousands of visitors to the Bradley campaign site had added their e-mail addresses to the campaign's mailing list. Such a treasure trove would be hard for an aspiring candidate to pass up, campaign consultants say. "I can tell you from personal experience as a GOP consultant in Alabama that mail lists are some of the most commonly stolen things on campaigns," read a posting from a reader who identified himself as David McElroy. "Both postal mail lists and e-mail lists tend to be copied by political operatives who find it passing through their hands. In my experience, it's at least as rampant as illegal software copying, simply because the lists are so valuable and the copying is so easy. … Many lists can be rented to campaigns (which don't have any idea of the list's origin in many cases) for thousands of dollars per campaign or use." In other words, e-mail addresses are fair game, no matter how, or from where, a campaign gathered them. Since information about potential supporters is the coin of the realm in campaigning, it's not hard to predict that the probing of voters' lives and the lax standards on the use of e-mail lists will continue to grow.

… While the Candidates and the Voters Yawn

If you look at *some* numbers, it appears that Americans turned out in force on the Internet during Election 2000. According to a study released February 18, 2001, by the well-regarded Pew Internet & American Life Project, for example, by the time the dispute over the

Florida recount got underway 48 percent of Internet users, or about fifty million Americans, were going to the Web to get news about the campaign. Only six months before, in May and June 2000, just a third of Internet users (34 percent) were looking for political news and information online, the study reported. Election news also drew a much more statistically significant audience on the Web in the 2000 campaign than it did in the 1996 campaign. According to a study released a month after the 2000 election by the Pew Research Center, the parent organization for the Internet & American Life Project, almost one in five Americans, or 18 percent, said they went online for political information in 2000 compared to only 4 percent in the previous presidential election year.

But were Americans really engaged in the election from an Internet perspective? Were the candidates? Some statistics may say yes, but other figures—among them Web site audience statistics—answer a resounding no.

Even though both the Republican and Democratic conventions were supposed to be high-tech wonders—with media and political sites offering "instant polls," nightly online forums, Webcams that roamed the convention floor, and chat rooms for the candidates—Net users fled the convention coverage. The average number of hits on MSNBC.com dropped almost 29 percent during the week of the Republican National Convention, while at the same time ABCNews.com suffered its lowest traffic in five months, *Variety* reported. The Democratic convention didn't improve the Web's fortunes: MSNBC.com lost about 700,000 visitors that week. When the Joan Shorenstein Center at Harvard University polled Americans who used the Internet during the GOP convention, it found that only one-third of them actively sought out convention information, and most of those who did so spent "just a few seconds" looking at it. "Americans had almost no interest in experiencing the convention over the Internet," the report, part of the Center's Vanishing Voter project, concluded.

Also, while Americans who regularly went online turned out to vote in higher numbers than members of the general population did during the 1992, 1994 and 1998 elections, those numbers did an about-face in 2000. In a poll conducted that fall among more than 4,000 online users, the Pew Center discovered that Internet regulars are now no longer more likely to vote than those who are not online. "Fully half of online election news consumers under age thirty say the information they received made them want to vote for or against a particular candidate," the Center noted when it released the study last December 3, 2000. *"Still, there has been no indication that the Internet is actually drawing more young people—or for that matter, more people of any age—into the political process.* Controlling for other factors related to participation, Internet users are no more likely to be engaged in the political process, and show no greater propensity to vote than do nonusers." [Italics added.]

Other organizations that studied how Americans used the Internet during the campaign season found similarly unappealing facts such as the following:

- Forty-four percent of the congressional candidates in the 2000 election did not have campaign Web sites, and those candidates who did have Web sites failed to offer the comparative content, campaign advertisements, and campaign finance information online users said they wanted, a study released in January 2001 by NetElection.org, a project of the Annenberg Public Policy Center of the University of Pennsylvania, reported.
- Online political advertisements often backfired and eroded a candidate's support among undecided voters in 2000, according to a study released around the same time by the Third Millennium group and Juno Online Services.
- Web sites devoted to political information crashed in droves either during or after the campaigns ended. BetterVote.com was sold in May 2000, Politics.com put its domain name up for auction six months later, and Voter.com, which was launched in November 1999 with millions of dollars in venture capital financing and the backing of over a thousand interest groups, shut down on February 6, 2001. Meanwhile, SpeakOut.com, a Web site originally designed as place for Netizens to debate public-policy issues and vote in public-opinion polls, changed its name and became an online marketing venture in January.

At the same time, high-tech issues figured somewhere between "not very interesting" and "b-o-r-i-n-g" as far as both presidential candidates were concerned. Some commentators attributed the campaigns' lack of interest in technology to the fact that Bush and Gore didn't really differ on those high-tech issues that did make it onto their respective radar screens. Both backed raising the number of visas for foreign high-tech workers and extending the current moratorium on taxation on the Internet, but such pressing questions as online privacy, the Digital Divide, or the legality of Napster and other "peer-to-peer" networks never made it into either candidate's speeches or onto the agenda for the presidential debates.

Other commentators suggest, however, that the lack of presidential campaign interest in high-tech issues stemmed instead from the unwillingness of either the Bush or Gore campaigns to alienate the computer industry, which split the millions of dollars it gave during the 2000 election cycle evenly between the two camps. In 1990, for example, the computer industry ranked fifty-fifth among industry campaign donors, with a total of $1.2 million split 48 percent to 52 percent among Democrats and Republicans, the Center for Responsive Politics has reported. A decade later, however, the computer industry had become the seventh largest industry campaign contributor in the country, spending almost $40 million on the 2000 election, split 52 percent to 47 percent between the Democrats and the GOP. "There's not much difference between Gore and Bush, unfortunately," Jeff Chester, president of the Washington-based Center for Media Education, told CNet News. When it comes to technology issues, "they're Tweedledum and Tweedledigital."

Chapter 10

On the Horizon

Maybe not this year, but in the next few years the Internet will completely turn political campaigns upside down.

—Sen. John McCain, R-Ariz., Republican presidential candidate, in the e-zine *Salon*, November 23, 1999

This history of electronic democracy began in 1994 with events that proved to be a turning point for the Internet. Seven years later, the Internet is at another critical juncture.

Technology is advancing so rapidly, scientists say, that within the foreseeable future the Internet as most Americans know it—a world accessible only through a computer, modem, and telephone wires—will disappear, to be replaced by a system of electronic connections so pervasive that the Internet will be a part of our homes, our appliances, our clothes, even—in some circumstances—our skin. If current experience is a model, the more "connected" our lives become, the more pressure we will face to conduct everything we do, including making political decisions, with ever-increasing speed. Instead of freeing us from quotidian concerns so that we can engage in the deliberative process, Internet technology could lead us to the edge of political disaster, making voting for President of the United States seem just as simple as ordering groceries online, and no more worthy of reflection.

But that doesn't have to happen. As we've seen, the Internet is the only communications medium that allows many people to talk to each other at the same time. No Internet user is forced to be a passive reader, listener, or viewer, particularly with the millions of chat rooms, mailing lists, free e-mail services, instant-messaging protocols, and streaming video outlets now available on the Web. It bears repeating: Unlike television, where the viewer can only absorb a message, not respond to it, the Internet promotes the exchange of ideas. Democracy is based on the interaction of citizens for the common good, and the Internet can be its most powerful instrument if it is put to proper use.

"The Internet in Everything"

As citizens, we will have to expand our concept of what "electronic democracy" means as the Internet undergoes a metamorphosis in the years to come. Already, telecommunications companies are moving toward making convergence a reality by rolling the pictures, sound, and text generated by cable television, telephones, and computer networks into one stream of data that can be delivered to the doorstep through a single wire or coaxial cable. Instead of four or five different electronic equipment systems in the den or family room, technology experts say, there will soon be only one system composed of a monitor, a keyboard, speakers, and a small "set top" box, resembling a cable converter, through which the user controls the data flow into the system.

That is only a small part of the changes Internet users face, however. According to the principle known in the high-tech industry as "Moore's Law," the capacity of the computer chip doubles about every eighteen months. Because of this rapid growth in computing power, Internet experts predict that, within the next decade, the Internet will be as big as today's telephone networks. Since the cost of processing information goes down as chips become more powerful, it will become economically feasible in the not-too-distant future to put computing power just about anywhere human imagination can find a use for it. Instead of bundling a laptop computer, a cell phone, a Palm Pilot, and a digital music player into a carrying case each morning, for example, busy Americans will pick up one machine that performs all these functions—plus serves as a portable television—and shove it into a coat pocket on the way out the door.

Some of this technology is already in the works and heading toward the consumer market. Palm Inc. is developing a wireless function that will allow consumers to encode their credit card information into a handheld device, where it can be beamed, along with a personal identification number or PIN, at a computer screen on a store counter when the consumer wants to make a purchase. XML, a programming language that allows Web sites to "talk" to each other, is under development at Microsoft and other high-tech companies. Eventually, it will enable a travel site, for example, to coordinate travel plans with the calendar on the traveler's handheld, check the airline's site to add his or her latest ticket to the frequent-flier mile tally, and notify his or her boss of the trip by automatically triggering e-mail on the desktop at work. If the flight is cancelled, the travel site will even be able to page the traveler with the information if the proper coordinates for the pager have been programmed in advance. Appliance makers are developing "smart" refrigerators with coders that scan new foodstuffs as they're added to the shelves, monitor the number of times an item is used, and switch on a warning light when a replacement is needed. There's even a miniscule chip powered by body heat now on the market that can track temperature, blood pressure, and other vital statistics and relay them back to a ground station using the Global Positioning System (GPS) network of satellites. While the privacy implications of this technology are enormous, it can also have beneficial uses for diabetics, heart patients and others with potentially life-threatening diseases, as well as for identification purposes in high-security jobs.

"My estimate is that there will be almost a billion devices on the Internet by the year 2006," Vinton G. Cerf, the co-creator of the TCP/IP protocol who is often called "the father of the Internet," said at an Internet Policy Institute gathering in late 1999. "The point is, the Internet is going to be in everything."

Living on Internet Time

A colleague active in the high-tech industry once had a sign on his office wall that read "Internet Speed Kills." As the Internet becomes more ubiquitous in our lives, it would be well to heed that warning.

Campaign staffers and online journalists already know something about the bewildering pace of life on Internet time. Demand for a continual stream of news and the growth of Web-based news sites have combined to push the now-twenty-four-hours news cycle to impossible—and sometimes laughable—proportions. In the early days of the presidential primaries, for example, Karen Hughes, press secretary for the Bush campaign, reportedly received a call from an Internet-based reporter who needed to post a story right away on the Web and wanted a quick response from Hughes's boss to his competitors' criticism on a campaign issue. The other candidates hadn't actually said anything yet, the reporter told Hughes, but he was certain they would and he wanted to get a Bush response while he awaited their calls. Around the same time the *Washington Post* reported that APBOnline, a Web site devoted to stories about crime and law enforcement, broke a story about a controversial crime exhibit the Seattle Art Museum was planning to stage. When the story hit the Internet, public reaction was so fierce and immediate that the museum cancelled the show that very day, and the APB reporter who wrote the original story posted a new item on the cancellation, all within less than twenty-four hours.

The *Post* called this phenomenon "minute-ly news" because it is driven by Web sites updated so frequently that news seems to be breaking "every single minute of every single day." But the forces that bring about the "minute-ly" nature of information on the Internet won't be confined to newscasts or campaign updates for long. As the Net becomes more ubiquitous, Americans will begin to see the information and services that shape their lives take on a minute-to-minute quality. When I took a recent business trip with a colleague to New York, for example, the train ran late, and as we rolled through Newark, we decided to have lunch before joining the rest of our group. My colleague logged on to the Internet on his wireless handheld, scanned the Zagat restaurant reviews for Manhattan, chose a restaurant, and made reservations on his cell phone. The same trend is happening in retailing, where such established firms as L.L. Bean now make instant-message connections with customer service available on their Web sites twenty-four hours a day, and in the automotive industry, where some higher-end cars now come equipped with GPS technology that can route the driver away from traffic jams and inclement weather at a moment's notice. These innovations certainly make our harried lives easier, but they also impart a sense of urgency that could be damaging to the political process. Imagine the effect last November 7, for instance, if voters in the Pacific Time zone were receiving instantaneous updates on the Florida vote tallies in the hour before their own polls closed. As beneficial as the Internet is for political debate and discourse, Americans must not make the mistake of substituting the information it provides for their own reasoned judgment on matters vital to the maintenance of the democratic system.

Will the Internet Be "As Big As TV?"

Guessing when the Internet will overtake television as *the* campaign medium has become something of a parlor game among reporters, political scientists, and high-tech types. Everyone wants to be the visionary who accurately predicts the moment when Americans are weaned away from the boob tube's standard fare of campaign photo-ops, over-produced commercials, and presidential "debates" as tightly scripted as any soap opera. In a 1998 speech at Harvard, for example, AOL founder Steve Case urged the audience to "work to ensure that the year 2000 is to the Internet what 1960 was to television: a coming of age." On the other hand noted political scientist Larry Sabato, of the University of Virginia, told the Associated Press around the same time that the Internet will not take precedence in the political process until Americans can vote online—a milestone that Sabato thinks is at least a decade away.

Certainly television has ceded some of its drawing power to the Internet. Often-visited Web sites now pull in as large a weekly audience as TV's ratings winners. More people, for example, visit Yahoo! each week than watch *The West Wing*, the popular series about the White House and a fictional inhabitant of the Oval Office. Even if a television program attracts twenty to thirty million viewers—as does the estimable *ER*, and its considerably less estimable competition, *Survivor*—that's a far cry from the mid-1950s when there were only three networks and half of America sat down every Sunday night to watch "Disneyland."

In comparison, more than 169 million Americans are online now. As that number grows, and as technological innovations continue to add to the visual and aural immediacy of the Internet, more and more voters will turn away from television during elections because they no longer find its one-dimensional, noninteractive presentations of candidates appealing. Consultant Phil Noble, founder of PoliticsOnline, for example, argues that modern American political history makes it inevitable that the Net will surpass television as the campaign medium of choice. In 1952, Noble says, fewer than 15 percent of American households had TV sets. The brand-new television networks covered the national conventions, but did not spend much time at all on the day-to-day progress of the presidential campaign. Four years later, about 40 percent of U.S. households had televisions, and both the Democratic National Committee and the Republican National Committee decided to spend some of the funds for the presidential campaigns on TV ads. Post-election research showed that the commercials influenced few voters. By 1960, however, televisions were in 90 percent of American households. "All of a sudden there was this handsome, virtually unknown Senator from Massachusetts who understood how to use the new medium. And he beat the current Vice President, who was beady-eyed, had a five o'clock shadow, and who never understood how to use television," Noble told me. "The same thing's going to happen with the Internet."

When that day comes, whether in two years or twenty, the balance of power will shift for candidates everywhere because the Internet dramatically reduces the expense of political communications. Even decked out in streaming video, Flash graphics, and pop-up windows with "always-on" access to the campaign, a Web site still costs less than a handful of last-minute television commercials and the prime-time slots in which to air them. E-mail costs a fraction of postal mail, and online fundraising is not only cheap but also remarkably effective, as we saw in the 2000 campaigns. Recruiting and managing volunteers and events online cuts down on campaign outlays for personnel, office space, and supplies.

All of these cost-savings mean that independent candidates, who often have meager campaign war chests, and third parties, whose pool of funds is usually only slightly bigger, will have a shot at leveling the playing field against candidates backed by special interests. Nothing could be healthier for the American political system.

"Generation Next" and the Coming of the Internet Age

Despite all the changes the Internet has wrought on the political process, it won't achieve a complete transformation for another ten to twelve years—when today's middle-schoolers reach adulthood.

Almost sixteen million children and teenagers go online monthly, according to Media Metrix, and more than half of that number are age twelve to seventeen. These are the kids who grew up with computers, to whom "56K" means a modem speed instead of a math problem, who know as much about RAM and MP3 as they know about skateboarding and the latest boy bands. They are part of "Generation Next" as identified by Pepsi-Cola marketers in a major recent ad campaign, and unlike their parents and grandparents, they consider the Internet just as natural a communications medium as the television, telephone, and radio.

In fact, anyone who has a computer and a preteen or teenager at home knows that this coming generation is just as likely to be online sending instant messages after school as watching TV or talking on the telephone. The Internet is a link to friends, a homework buddy, an entertainment center, a shopping mall, and, last but not least, an information resource for Generation Next. More than two-thirds of them go online at least once a week and 35 percent report that they're online "almost every day," according to a joint study by the Kaiser Family Foundation and National Public Radio. The constant exposure to electronic communications has made cyberspace friendly territory for many in this age group. Where their grandparents are print-oriented, read for pleasure, and are generally flummoxed by the Internet, and their parents—the first generation to grow up with television—are visually oriented, can't live without cable TV, and sometimes struggle to get their laptops to work, today's ten- to seventeen-year-olds read, watch, and learn from the Internet without giving the entire process a second thought.

What this means is that the members of Generation Next are likely to come of age expecting to conduct their political business online just as they conduct the other facets of their lives online. In an ABC News survey in late 2000, only 19 percent of Americans age sixty-five and older supported Internet voting but a whopping 60 percent of the young adults age eighteen to thirty-four said they would vote online if they could. Shortly thereafter, the Pew Internet & American Life Project reported that more than half the adults in this country don't have Internet access, and that 57 percent of that group doesn't want access because they consider the online world dangerous. Almost the same number said they don't use the Internet because they don't think they're missing anything by staying away from it. "Most of the strongest Internet holdouts are older Americans, who are fretful about the online world and often don't believe it can bring them any benefits. In contrast, a substantial majority of those under thirty who are not currently online say they plan to get access," Pew reported. As long as a significant percentage of the over-fifty population continues to hold the Internet at arm's length, online communications won't become ubiquitous. But by 2010 or 2015, as the ranks of the older generation thin and Generation Next reaches adulthood, the Internet's real transformation of American politics will begin.

ABOUT THE AUTHOR

Graeme Browning has been a writer, reporter, and editor for more than twenty years. She covered technology policy for *National Journal*, and was also a reporter for the *Washington Post*, *The* (Baltimore) *Sun*, the *Chicago Sun-Times*, and United Press International. She was a member of the editorial board of *The* (Nashville) *Tennessean*, and legal affairs reporter for the ABC affiliate in Nashville.

Browning served as editorial director of the Internet Policy Institute in Washington, D.C., and is currently Associate Editor for *Federal Computer Week* magazine, in Falls Church, Va. She is a graduate of Vanderbilt Law School and also the author of *If Everybody Bought One Shoe: American Capitalism in Communist China* (1988). She lives in Bethesda, Md., with her daughter.

Index

B

C

D

E

F

G

I

J

K

L

M

N

S

T

More CyberAge Books from Information Today, Inc.

Internet Blue Pages

The Guide to Federal Government Web Sites, 2001-2002 Edition

Compiled by Laurie Andriot

Internet Blue Pages (*IBP*) is the leading guide to federal government information on the Web. *IBP 2001–2002* includes over 1,800 annotated agency listings arranged in U.S. Government Manual style to help you find the information you need. Entries include agency name and URL, function or purpose of selected agencies, and links from agency home pages. With double the coverage of the previous edition, *IBP* now includes federal courts, military libraries, Department of Energy libraries, Federal Reserve banks, presidential libraries, national parks, and Social Security offices. A companion Web site features regularly updated agency links.

2000/464 pp/softbound/ISBN 0-910965-43-9 $34.95

Naked in Cyberspace

How to Find Personal Information Online, 2nd Edition

By Carole A. Lane
Foreword by Beth Givens

In this fully revised and updated second edition of her bestselling guide, author Carole A. Lane surveys the types of personal records that are available on the Internet and online services. Lane explains how researchers find and use personal data, identifies the most useful sources of information about people, and offers advice for readers with privacy concerns. You'll learn how to use online tools and databases to gain competitive intelligence, locate and investigate people, access public records, indentify experts, find new customers, recruit employees, search for assets, uncover criminal records, conduct genealogical research, and much more. *Naked in Cyberspace* is the ultimate handbook for anyone who needs information about people. A companion Web directory provides links to more than 1,000 important reader resources.

2002/586 pp/softbound/ISBN 0-910965-50-1 $29.95